S FR.
CH

CLASSIC *f*M LIFELINES

FRANZ SCHUBERT

AN ESSENTIAL GUIDE TO HIS LIFE AND WORKS

STEPHEN JACKSON

PAVILION

First published in Great Britain in 1996 by
PAVILION BOOKS LIMITED
26 Upper Ground, London SE1 9PD

Copyright © Pavilion Books Ltd 1996
Front cover illustration © The Hulton Deutsch Collection 1996

Edited and designed by Castle House Press, Llantrisant, South Wales
Cover designed by Bet Ayer

A CIP catalogue record for this book is available
from the British Library

ISBN 1 85793 987 5

Set in Lydian and Caslon
Printed and bound in Great Britain by Mackays of Chatham

2 4 6 8 10 9 7 5 3 1

This book can be ordered direct from the publisher.
Please contact the Marketing Department.
But try your bookshop first.

Contents

ACKNOWLEDGMENTS

To my parents, and my music teacher Carol Walker, for putting me on the right path; and to Edward Greenfield, for giving me the courage to see it through.

Thanks are due too – as ever – to Richard at BMG, Harriet at Warner, Katherine and Kerry at EMI, Celia at Hyperion and Carole at Sony for their indefatigable support, without which this project would not have been possible.

A NOTE FROM THE EDITORS

A biography of this type inevitably contains numerous references to pieces of music. The paragraphs are also peppered with 'quotation marks', since much of the tale is told through reported speech.

Because of this, and to make things more accessible for the reader as well as easier on the eye, we decided to simplify the method of typesetting the names of musical works. Conventionally this is determined by the nature of the individual work, following a set of rules whereby some pieces appear in italics, some in italics and quotation marks, others in plain roman type and others still in roman and quotation marks.

In this book, the names of all musical works are simply set in italics. Songs and arias appear in italics and quotation marks.

CHAPTER I
SCHUBERT'S VIENNA AND THE EARLY YEARS (1797–1813)

- ♦ *Schubert's Vienna*
- ♦ *A precocious musical talent*
- ♦ *Adolescence*
- ♦ *Early compositions – the First Symphony*

chubert was born on 31 January 1797, the suburban Viennese son of a family of schoolteachers. He would die as he had lived – as yet another composer struggling to be more than an amateur, whose music was outsold many times over by Hummel's. As a creative force he left as many successors as Mozart did – which is to say, none. Rachmaninov, questioned in the early years of our century, did not know of a single piano sonata by Schubert. Fifty years before, only sheer tact had salvaged the neglected manuscript of the '*Unfinished*' *Symphony* from oblivion. By that time, its composer had been in the Währing Cemetery for decades.

Like some magical and insidious alchemy, Schubert exists outside the tradition he inherited. His influence has worked subtly on generations of composers, each of whom has stumbled on the modernity of what he has to say: seeping into our consciousness not only of music's potential but of our human predicament. For Schubert has done as much as any artist to crystallize our sense of self, and he explored with prophetic intensity a fusion of poetry and the heightened capabilities of a singing voice that was to release the later nineteenth century's artistic interrogation of the limits of experience: of what it might be possible for us ever to say, or to know.

You never seem to hear Schubert's music in a television advertisement. His is not a creative language that lends itself to soundbites and domesticated lifestyles. It fosters little of his predecessors' overweening urge to explain themselves, the regulated good sense of the Enlightenment. It lacks the need to preach, it carries no burden of oratory. From the majestic clockwork of high classicism we have received (as Schubert did) a vocabulary of known formalities and unambiguous manoeuvres, which we can recognize at a glance, which we can assimilate into a background where emotion is as safe as the wallpaper. Tackle Schubert, and things are no longer so certain. In his world, surface formalities – however elegant or lucid they may appear – serve as an entry-point for an act of deeper and private scrutiny, where what a composer thinks he knows is there to be subverted or expanded into a luminous perspective where meanings themselves are freshly crafted and constantly redefined.

It is a cipher for each listener to find and make sense of for himself: and it offers apt introspection for an age weary of dogmatic statements. We find ourselves in an era as much preoccupied as the early 19th century was with the spread of sexual disease and the violation of innocence; a pre-millennial circumspection, it seems, for which Schubert's triumph over his fate and his own meagre life seems increasingly to the point. Understood in its true light, his music comes as a revelation that stands beyond cultural history and which throws down an emotional challenge that is as new and as personal for us as it was for Brahms, Schumann, Bruckner, Mahler, Dvořák, Stravinsky, Britten, Wolf. It is music propelled by ardent intensity, by an appetite and melancholy and lacerating nostalgia, which come wholly from within.

Strange it is that Schubert, the least gregariously jovial of great Viennese composers, was the only one to be born there. It is a place he made in his own image, because the portrait we have of it comes from the traditional minuets, waltzes and *Ländler*, which he took and changed into something new. This is the mirage Schumann fell for when he described the *Ninth Symphony*:

> *Schubert's* Symphony, *with the clear romantic spirit that quickens it, brings the city more vividly before my eyes today than ever before, and makes me understand once again how it is that such*

*works come to be born in surroundings such as these . . . with
its St Stephen's spire, its lovely women, its public pageantry,
encircled by the countless hoops of the Danube and stretching
across the verdant plain which climbs gently towards higher
and still higher mountains. . . .*

For a more accurate appraisal we must turn to Johann Pezzl's
Sketch of Vienna, which covered the years 1786–90. Everything
interested him: the overwhelming stink of unwashed crowds, the
glee with which good people flocked to watch bears being baited
and criminals branded before they were broken, shrieking, upon
a wheel: streets filled with mistresses and those 'of easy virtue'.
As for the lovely ladies, foreign visitors noted that countesses
behaved like courtesans and courtesans like countesses; the cheap
and innumerable dance-halls were thinly-disguised brothels.

Politically the situation worsened in Schubert's lifetime, as
the reforms of Joseph II were swept away by Prince Metternich's
autocracy. In 1820, with student societies banned, the composer
found himself arrested at what one can only call the wrong sort
of party. He was released as harmless – a luckier fate than befell
those who were banished for life on that occasion. The public was
fickle towards the arts, responsive only to sentimental fads and
virtuosity of the most meretricious kind. It was something Mozart
had discovered to his recent and bitter cost.

Yet Schubert was a lucky man. He was born at a remarkable
time for lyric verse, and unlike Mozart or Haydn or Beethoven –
all of whom had been unable to transcend the limitations of
conventionally ornate songwriting – he was profoundly attuned
to what was happening. He could root out a talent for poetry not
only within his circle of friends, but from the remotest fringes of
the German-speaking world. He discovered the early Romantics
(Heine, Rückert, Platen, Uhland) and immortalized them: he
followed Goethe along new paths into passion instead of rhetoric,
feeling instead of either reason or bathos: he championed the
world-view that led beyond music to Goya and Turner.

The origins of a tradition that comes to opulent, Romantic
flower in Strauss's '*Four Last Songs*' lie in the cheap musical
browsings of Schubert's childhood. There he found Zumsteeg,
the south German composer who in 1791 had set Ossian and
revealed for the first time the potential of song as a vehicle for

dramatic and psychological revelation. Two north Germans composing around 1800, Reichardt and Zelter, explored in their own *Lieder* a new freedom of form, an expressive richness of mood. All this was anathema to the sophisticated Viennese, who trounced it into obscurity. But Schubert knew of it, and it created the live wire to which he could bring his own peculiar and incandescent charge. Rather seldom does the history of the arts have to do with a torch being passed from one illustrious bearer to another. It lies in the tiny quirks and accidents that one individual can grasp and lift into greatness.

A PRECOCIOUS MUSICAL TALENT

Franz Peter was the twelfth child of Franz Theodor Schubert, who had moved to Vienna from Neudorf in Moravia. In 1786 Franz *père* was appointed master to the Trivial School No.12 Himmel-pfort-grund, eighteen months after he had married Maria Elizabeth Vietz, the daughter of a Silesian locksmith. She too had come to the city to seek her fortune, and was working as a cook: a gentle woman, it was said, loved and respected by everyone. Young Franz was born in the Liechtental district, on the fringe of the country-side, where poverty gave a family little chance of a quick rise in the scheme of things. It was an affectionate family even so, and Schubert got on well with his father, despite the older man's strictness. But his special intimacy was with Maria, from whom he inherited his quiet reflective manner, his imagination, and his easy-going ways. She died in 1812.

The western world, at Franz Peter's birth, might have seemed on the brink of a new era in political turbulence and social opportunity. Seventeen days earlier, French troops had beaten the Austrians at Aricole and Rivoli. The American War of Independence was barely over, and in 1805 Napoleon marched through Vienna – a little Corsican upstart who had robbed the Habsburgs of most of their empire. In this changing order, a teacher was no longer the ignorant, despised Baculus of the eighteenth century. He moved in higher circles and entered into the intellectual activities of the middle-class, while preserving a level of patriot-ism unknown to the garrulous *nouveaux riches*. His prospects for promotion were in no sense harmed by religious awe – by devo-tion, as was the case in the Schubert household. For this was an empire that moved at the speed of a cantering horse, and in 1797 the shadow of Napoleon was still far away. In life's daily rhythms, an old Imperial order reigned supreme.

Vienna stood as the city of Gluck, Beethoven, Mozart and Haydn. It was the melting-pot of European races and culture in the prime of its greatest epoch. A schoolmaster was expected to be competent in music, and the Schuberts' house echoed with it. Franz had lessons in piano from his father, and his first taste of the violin from his older brother Ignaz. That he outstripped them both was plain, but Schubert wrote his first music for the family quartet. When his father's hands fumbled on the cello, Franz would smile and venture, 'Sir, there must be a mistake somewhere!'

In his eighth year he was sent for lessons in singing and counterpoint with Michael Holzer, the local organist, whose choir Schubert joined. Towards the end of his life Franz Senior remembered that Holzer had confessed to doing little more than while away time: 'If I wanted to teach him something new – he had already mastered it. Often I stared in silent astonishment. I could not give him any real instruction, only talk with the lad and quietly admire him.' His reward was the dedication of Schubert's *C major Mass*, in 1816.

Under Holzer's care Schubert's violin-playing earned him a local reputation, and in 1808 he was well-placed to take advantage of an advertisement in the *Vienna Gazette*:

> *At the end of the present school year a place for soprano will become available at the Imperial College. Whoever wishes to obtain this place for his son has to satisfy the Directorate of the said College, where an examination is to be held on 1 October, that the candidate is fit to enter the first Latin class, has a good voice, and has been well-trained in singing.*

Schubert's audition was held before Antonio Salieri, a friend of Beethoven, mentor to Haydn, Mozart's rival, and now *Kapellmeister* to the Emperor. A week later, the announcement of his acceptance was received.

The college was the principal Viennese boarding school for commoners. It was a place of iron rations and, in the winter, bitter cold. In an affectionate letter to his brothers, Franz had to bring himself to write:

You'll know from your own experience that there are times when one could certainly do with a roll and a few apples, particularly when one has to wait eight and a half hours between a moderate-sized midday meal and a wretched sort of supper. This constant longing has become more and more insistent, and the time has come when I must do something about it. The few Groschen that Father gave me vanished into thin air in the first few days, so what am I going to do for the rest of the time? They who hope upon Thee shall not be put to shame. *St Matthew, 3 : 4. How would it be, then, if you were to let me have a few Kreuzer each month? You wouldn't notice them, and they would make me happy and contented in my cell.*

The tutors were men in holy orders and their boarders, about a hundred and thirty of them, either scholars at the grammar school or students at the university. Music was a compulsory subject for choristers, but the principal, Dr Innocenz Lang, was an enthusiastic musical amateur and he encouraged all scholars to practise the art. Schubert played quartets regularly, and his latest songs were celebrated by the school as enthusiastically as any sporting achievement. Yet his tastes and talents set him apart, for as the surgeon Georg Eckel later recalled:

Schubert's life was one of inner, spiritual thinking, and was seldom expressed in words but I would say, almost entirely in music. Even with his intimates he was shy and uncommunicative ... Schubert almost always spent the leisure hours we were allowed in the music room, and generally alone. Even on the walks which pupils took together he mostly kept apart, walking thoughtfully along with lowered eyes and with hands behind his back, drumming with his fingers (as if on keys), completely absorbed in his own thought.

A young university student, Josef von Spaun, had formed a students' orchestra, which was conducted by Vaclav Ruzicka, a peripatetic master. By the time of Schubert's arrival, its excellence was sufficient to tackle Beethoven's first two symphonies, which were then the last word in difficulty and daring. Schubert joined the violins and Spaun, impressed by his rhythm and wholehearted surrender to the music, took Franz under his wing.

Their friendship lasted for the rest of Schubert's life. One of Spaun's first acts, when Franz confessed that he could not afford music paper, was to provide him with all he needed.

When after two years' absence Spaun returned, he discovered Schubert conducting the orchestra in the absence of Ruzicka, who had found himself nonplussed by the rate at which his disciple had absorbed all instruction. Their arrangement had the blessing of Salieri, whom Schubert visited twice a week for lessons in harmony and counterpoint. Salieri's interest had been roused by the song '*Hagars Klage*' (D5). Promptly he unleashed a flood of penny-dreadful ballads from his pupil, but amongst them is a setting of Schiller's poem *Der Jünglinge am Bache* that must lay claim to being the first real Schubert song: lithe and subtle in its lengths of phrase.

Schubert's last year at the college was 1813, and his wealth of compositions attested to the quality and variety of what he had learned: a Mozartean *Quartet in E flat* (D87), German dances, settings of Metastasio, Hölty, Matthisson. In the autumn Spaun took him to see his first operas, and in a half-empty theatre (whilst the rest of Vienna was feting Rossini) Schubert fell under the spell of Gluck's *Iphigénie and Euride*. Perhaps drawing on *Die Zauberflöte* as his exemplar, he began work on his own three-act opera *Des Teufels Lustschloss* (D84), taking leave from lessons until he could present its fully orchestrated score to an astonished Salieri. The master's criticisms were heeded, for a revised version is dated five months after the first.

The highlight of 1813 is the *D major First Symphony* (D82), which Schubert finished on 28 October. This is music of ordered and festive abundance. And if, motifically, it struggles to be more than a pastiche of a young man's models (Mozart in its organization, Beethoven for its themes) the sheer sound is already and inimitably voluptuous. Nobody else, you feel, could write dialogues for woodwind quite like this. It is, as the critic Maurice Brown has said, the consummation of absorbed years and of living contact with an orchestra: it is his justification for the future.

CHAPTER 2
A RELUCTANT SCHOOLMASTER
(1813–15)

- ♦ *Career as a teacher*
- ♦ *Settings of Goethe*
- ♦ *The Schubertiads*

During 1813, Schubert's future at the College hung in the balance. Devotion to music meant that his progress in Latin and mathematics had been precarious, and some way had to be found to keep him in an environment where his talents could prosper. As it happened, an annual scholarship (the Meerfield Endowment) fell vacant, and it was decided to recommend Schubert for it. The judgment was up to Emperor Francis himself, and he approved the 16-year-old's application while he was engaged in the campaign to drive Napoleon deep within the borders of France.

But it was the elder Schubert who decided his son's future, and Spaun remembers violent quarrels when Franz was informed that he would have to leave his composing for the evenings. In November, Schubert enrolled at St Anna's Teacher Training College, where he marked time until his father took him on for £8 a year in the autumn of 1814. It was a pittance of a salary, but sons were there to save wages; and the Liechtental school now had 300 pupils. Franz's lot was to teach six-year-olds their alphabet, and they remembered him as uncomprehending and bored. His own reminiscences were illuminating:

> *It's true that the children irritated me whenever I tried to create, and I lost the idea. Naturally I would beat them up.*

After a month's stagnation he took up his pen with renewed zeal. He had paused, if he'd known it, on the threshold of a staggering creative breakthrough, which would produce four hundred works before he left his parents' home in two years' time. His countrymen, euphoric at Napoleon's exile and the Congress of Vienna (it made reliably dissolute entertainment before the country relapsed into greater despotism than ever before) discovered a fondness for Beethoven's *Fidelio*. Schubert went to see it and was gripped by a renewed mania for writing opera. He realized that there was no success to be had with *Der Teufels Lustschloß*, but within a fortnight during May 1815 he whipped up the breezy *Der vierjährige Posten* (D190) from the tale of a soldier who falls in love with the daughter of a village judge.

Over twelve days in July he drafted an epic of melodramatic banality, *Fernando*. Then, until the end of August, he was busy with *Claudine von Villa Bella* (D239). By New Year's Day he had finished his humorous and charming *Die Freunde von Salamanka* (D326).

There was more besides. A buckshot approach, but in *Claudine* it threw up a masterpiece. At least, so we think; for only the first act has survived. The rest, in one of those unfortunate lapses of understanding, was used by Josef Hüttenbrenner's servants for lighting fires. Naturally it was with him for safekeeping.

Schubert found greater success in his liturgical music. The Vienna Congress coincided with the centenary celebrations of the Liechtental Church. Schubert's *Mass in F* (D105) was performed in Salieri's presence as part of the festivities in October 1814, and the soprano solos were sung by Therese Grob, a mill-owner's daughter with a sweet lyric voice. Schubert loved her with quiet sincerity, and only abandoned his hopes of marrying her three years later when his prospects of joining the middle class were in tatters. By that time Holzapfel, his confidant, had talked him out of 'this ridiculous infatuation'. But it is not fortuitous that his first stroke of greatness in the vocal domain, depicting the shattering of a young woman's dreams, came ten days after her performance: 'When he is not with me, I am as though dead.' The Mass itself is a work spun out of light: free, sure and gracefully dignified.

Schubert notes with pride, above the Allegro of his D112 *Quartet* : 'Completed in four-and-a-half hours'. At its best it is a piece worthy of young Mendelssohn, but there is no greater tribute to Schubert's new-found facility and sense of adventure than the second of his completed symphonies, the *B flat* (D125), which he began on 10 December 1814. Brahms loved this work for, as he said, its genuine delight. Again, allusions to Mozart are within it – the *E flat* and *G minor Symphonies* – and to *Prometheus* as well as to Beethoven's own *Second Symphony*. None of these origins prefigures a young man's plunge into the middle of life: his new-found energy and bite. Brian Newbould understood that the *B flat major* is a consequence of fresh reflection and self-questioning, where the power of dissonance is harnessed to create pace and tensile strength. As Alfred Einstein notes of the *Presto* finale, 'It is a piece of symphonic frivolity in sonata form, full of dynamic surprises, dropping off to sleep, as it were, and then waking up with a start.' If the *Third* is the neatest of his early symphonies, the *Second* contains the most fertile dues to Schubert's future.

Exasperated in the schoolroom, Schubert frequented local taverns and brought home new male friends – to the displeasure of his father, who perhaps already sensed that something about them was not right. At lodgings in the Wipplingerstraße a meeting was arranged by Spaun between young Franz and Johann Mayrhofer, a taciturn and mysogynistic lawyer, ten years older than Schubert, whose poetry – revealing as it does the conflict between ideals of the spirit and the actualities of life – was to draw noble songs from the composer for the rest of his career. In 1836 Mayrhofer's second attempt at suicide would prove successful when he threw himself from an upper window of the building where he worked as state Censor; but he was one of Schubert's few supporters to glimpse the true dimensions of a genius, and he declared that none of his own verses seemed any good until Schubert set them.

Schubert was to use more of Mayrhofer's work than of any poet except Goethe. Already he had set *Am See* (D124), a wistful remembrance of heroic deeds. But then, 1814 was Schubert's first great year of song: unleashing a Shakespearean canvas of characters, emancipating single-handed the piano from slavish accompaniment to a dramatic player in the role of interlocutor, combatant, adversary, commentary, and propulsive narrative force. The *Lied*, for Schubert, has fluidity and intimate depth, newness and courage. His sense of movement and the possibilities of a melodic line, his unique awareness of changing key, his master storyteller's relish for timing and shifting nuance: all these gave the *Lied* a power and a poignancy that had previously seemed inconceivable.

In April 1814 alone he composed thirteen settings of Friedrich von Matthisson, whose collected works had been published three years before. In them Schubert found reflected his own artistic vistas: country scenes set in a sentimental light, ecstatic love, emotional remembrance, the anticipation of death. Yet in one poet alone did Schubert found an intellect equal to his own, whose work he could fuse and expand into a totality greater than the sum of its parts. It was Goethe, and on 19 October Schubert plucked '*Gretchen am Spinnrade*' (D118) from *Faust*. Margaret, bewitched by Faust's love, sits at her spinning-wheel and contemplates the possibility of her ruin: '*Meine Ruh ist hin, Mein Herz ist schwer.*' The piano's churning semiquavers are more that the droning monotony of physical motion, more too than wretched perplexity. They are the distillation of the moment at which a life is thrown into relief and meets its reckoning.

'The birth of German song', '*Gretchen*' has been called. In the space of four minutes unfolds a drama which, if Schubert had written nothing else, would ensure his immortality.

ANNUS MIRABILIS: 1815

Schubert wrote eight other songs the day he set '*Gretchen*', but 1815 produced even greater profusion. Otto Eric Deutsch's catalogue of his works lists two hundred within twelve months: Masses and a splendid *Magnificat*, a string quartet, dances, fragments of piano sonatas. Above all he wrote *Lieder* – one hundred and fifty of them.

The notion of Schubert as a divinely gifted clairvoyant, scribbling music in a daydream, is one of many myths. He was breaking down the boundaries of song, with nobody to guide him: he knew when he had failed, and he returns to a poet – perhaps years later – until he finds a solution that covers each facet of the words, answers every challenge. The secret comes when he fixes on a melodic or rhythmic cell, which encompasses the poem's essence, and yet which is flexible enough to adapt to a changing narrative. Gretchen's spinning wheel is an instance. Before Schubert, songs had been strophic (that is to say, a repeated melody for verse after verse: the formula of hymns and ballads). Schubert's first songs follow this scheme, yet increasingly he finds some means of higher liberation which will open up something as great as theatre on an epic scale, something as private as a stream of consciousness.

Why did he set so much Goethe, following that revelatory reading of *Faust* ? Because, as Goethe says, 'The most original men are not original because they tell us something absolutely new, but because they tell us things in a way in which they were never told before.' The compression of Goethe's emotional environment – transparent, classical in form and formal restraint yet profoundly individual – draws similar truth from the composer. Goethe's voice informs Schubert's, whether he is setting Goethe or not. As Dietrich Fischer-Dieskau writes, 'Schubert found everything in Goethe's poems that he tried to express in music. Clarity of thought, unequivocal expression, deep sensitivity, imaginative language.'

Spaun tells how, one afternoon towards the end of 1815, he and Mayrhofer visited Schubert to find him glowing with excitement as he read aloud *Erlkönig*, Goethe's ballad of a child abducted by the king of demons on a stormy night. Briefly Schubert paced to and fro and then down he sat, committing the setting straight to paper. Since his father had no piano, the three friends hurried to the Imperial College where it was performed a few hours later, and twice encored. After Ruzicka had approvingly played it through, Schubert accompanied Randhartinger, a fourteen-year-old plucked from the audience, until its hammering octaves exhausted his hands. In triumph, Schubert was presented with reams of music paper.

The song is a masterpiece of scene-painting. Instantly we are made witnesses to a dreadful and fevered hallucination, a nightmare that unfolds with the stride of galloping hooves. The Erlking's seductive insinuations, whispered promises of golden cloth and fairy playmates, are made part of surmounting musical modulation, at whose climax one key leaps to another in a despairing frenzy. Too late the father realizes what has happened, and his boy is dead.

It is the highlight of a year's memorable achievement. Already Schubert had grappled with the poetry of Goethe's strange novel *Wilhelm Meisters Lehrjahre*, which had been published in

1795–96. Its verses are songs sung by a mysterious figure, the Harper, and by Mignon, the Italian waif who turns out to be the Harper's daughter, offspring of incestuous love. It includes the most admired poem in German literature, the elegiac '*Kennst du das Land?*' ('*Do you know the land where the lemon-trees blossom?*'), which Schubert set as well as anyone since: '*Mignon und der Harfner*' held Schubert in its spell for the rest of his life, and he set it five times, but his 1815 version is the best.

Better still is '*An Mignon*' ('*Alone, my tears flow, but in company I'll keep cheerful*'): '*Am Fluße*', set on the same day, brims with sweet pathos: '*Meers Stille*' is a masterly evocation of deathly calm at sea. Yet three Goethe songs from 1815 stand supreme. '*Heidenröslein*' (D257), the story of a wild rose which stabs the lover who plucks it, has a bucolic simplicity and freshness that elevates folksong to art. '*Rastlose Liebe*' (D222) is a surge of pure feeling, as fine as anything in Romanticism's liberation of painting at the same time. Above all there is '*Nähe des Geliebten*' (D162, 'Nearness of the Beloved': 'I think of you when with the shimmer of sunlight the bright sea gleams'), where the slow palpitation of the piano's chords summons a sense of delight made more boundless by its poised containment and grace.

But there were other poets to set. Friedrich Klopstock, who anticipates the *Sturm und Drang* ('storm and stress') period of German literature, had found fame with his epic *The Messiah* – and in '*Dem Unendlichen*' (D291) Schubert matches him in stately religious fervour.

Then there was Klopstock's pupil, Schiller. '*Des Mädchens Klage*' is pure pathos again, the singer's voice rising above pulsating triplets: '*Hektors Abschied*' is as stately as the 'farewell' of a classical hero demands: '*Das Geheimnis*' is a love song of pristine delicacy and tenderness, anticipating Schumann. Its only concession to Schubert's youth is that he feels he has to adapt to every verse. Later he would gain the shrewd economy of an old hand.

In the autumn, Schubert was introduced to Maurice von Schwind, a dilettante poet studying law, who had heard his songs and had come to Vienna to seek their composer. He found Schubert in his schoolroom, correcting exercises. The two of them were the same age, and the cultured, worldly man urged Schubert to abandon the drudgery of teaching and devote himself to composition. In 1815, then, we see in place the personnel of the Schubertiads: those musical gatherings of friends before whom the composer could try out his latest offerings. The name is their own, and the offerings were not only his; if one of their new poems appealed to him, he might set it straightaway.

His friends occupy a unique place in Schubert's life. They were his supporters, critics, a source of stimulus who, as aristocrats of a new and literate social class (many of its members educated at university) were able to introduce him to the shifting ideas and cultural currents that gave first impetus to the new Romantic age. As Spaun recalled, 'Through Schubert we all became friends and brothers.' When Schubert did not live at home, he lived with them and they talked about him, spreading his name. Joseph Wechsberg made a perceptive judgment of the impression they leave in their memoirs and drawings:

> *A relaxed crowd, always singing and dancing, and their girls were pretty in their high-waisted long dresses. They would make excursions in the countryside or sit in wine gardens; they convey the image of a Biedermeier idyll. No wonder, since most of the paintings were made much later when the artists remembered their earlier idyllic years with a sharp sense of nostalgia.*

This was the era nonetheless when, as Abraham a Sancta Clara could report, 'music resounded from noblemen's houses and courtyards.' There was a piano in every cultured home and *Hausmusik* (chamber music) in every drawing room. The public at large enjoyed the *Harmoniemusik* of military bands in streets and squares, the string ensembles of Johann Strauss the Elder, harp players in the Prater, organ-grinders everywhere, and musical clocks on many buildings. After the charades and high jinks of an evening's Schubertiad, there would be instrumental pieces to write for bands of cultured dilettantes. One of this number and a friend from Imperial College days, Albert Stadler, copied out until 1817 every one of Schubert's songs in his own hand, rescuing several for posterity. Another recruit from 1815 is Franz von Schober, a flamboyant and epicurean lawyer who later became private secretary to Liszt: again an aspiring poet, maligned by other friends, with whom Schubert nonetheless shared his most intense confidences. At the age of 60 he married a firecracking intellectual.

It is interesting to speculate what a Schubertiad of 1815 might have been like. Pudgy little Franz's latest and hearty setting of Körner's war-ballads, perhaps: glorious songs drawn from Hölty (*'An den Mond'*, D193) and Kosegarten (*'Die Mondnacht'*, D238): Ossian's Celtic dirges, and of course Mayrhofer, who tempered Schiller's enthusiasm for classical antiquity with Ossian's gloom. But the compass of Schubert's thought was expanding beyond any of it. The first two symphonies had unearthed possibilities but they were derivative and prolix: they needed geniality, suavity, polish, finesse. These Schubert was ready to provide. His *Third Symphony* (D200) was written between 24 May and 19 July. The dates obscure its energy of inspiration, for between them he set the manuscript aside to write *'Fernando'* and much else. Most of the symphony was dashed off in eight days.

We might guess as much, to judge by the overflowing spontaneity of the finale, but not from the serene confidence and craftsmanship of the conception as a whole. Its spirit is rococo, and enchanting. True, the slow movement is Haydnesque; but Schubert's voice throughout is clear and crisp in its organization of matters-at-hand. The snapping dotted crochets of his *'Great' C major Symphony* have their origin in the first movement of D200: Schubert's buffo *Presto vivace* anticipates the finale of his *D minor String Quartet* a decade later. It has been claimed that, if Schubert took to the *Lied* like a duck to water, in orchestral music he had to learn how to swim. He learned quickly. In this second *D major Symphony* there is a tightly integrated discourse, a level of repartee, which reveals at every stage how deftly Schubert has learnt to make a stimulus as natural as breathing into a symphony. And this is what allows the music to smile.

As for *'Erlkönig'* (D328), it remained a *cause célèbre* among Schubert's friends for the remainder of his life. In 1816 Spaun submitted it among a collection of Goethe settings to the poet himself, asking for a dedication so that the songs might be published with his blessing. It was returned without a word.

CHAPTER 3
THE PROMISE OF FREEDOM
(1816–18)

♦ A period of indecision
♦ Schubert leaves home
♦ Meeting with Johann Vogl

The year following '*Erlkönig*' was one of miserable indecision for
Schubert, and by 1816 the time had come for him to leave the
family home. His father, primly religious, supported Metternich's crackdown on the arts, letters and for that matter
travelling arrangements of anyone who might have been tainted
by a whiff of subversion – any opponent of state or church who
could be unmasked by the network of secret agents which per-
meated every street-corner. Arrest was arbitrary, unlimited: and
Mayrhofer's publication of a magazine for enlightened ideas,
Contributions to Education for Young People, was enough to arouse
suspicion. These were the circumstances under which Franz
himself, out for the night with his friend Johann Senn, would in
a couple of years be detained without charge. As Mayrhofer wrote,
'Schubert's melodies will disperse the gloom which surrounds us
in these difficult days'.

Goethe's rejection of Spaun's letter must have been a stupe-
fying blow, and at the beginning of the year Schubert's application
for the post of Music Director at the College at Laibach had been
turned down despite Salieri's advocacy. In June 1816 he began to
keep a diary (seldom the priority of a happy person) in which he
notes his first composition for money. Other entries are desultory,
fragmented, incidental. The companionship of his friends began
to shine like a beacon upon an empty life, and by December, he
was living at Schober's family rooms in the Lands-krongasse, on the

understanding that he might contribute to his upkeep when he could afford to.

Much of Schubert's music over the long months reflects his disorientation. It treads water inconsequentially, as the work of occasional composers is liable to do, but there are fields in which he progresses with a vengeance. Hoping to advance himself in a fashionable sphere (which, had he realized, was already on the wane) he attempted seven piano sonatas in 1817, meaning perhaps to publish them with a single opus number as older composers had done. Beethoven's influence is tangible in the contemplative *E minor* (D566) and the *E flat* (D568), where coy and luscious tenderness co-exist. But Schubert is coming of age on his own terms, and he experiments freely with both form and medium. In the slow movement of the Haydnesque *A flat* (D557) and several lovely fragments, Schubert contrives a masterpiece within its conventions: it is, as Alfred Einstein says, music that has fallen from heaven.

Schubert's lyricism has no need of formal expositions, no need of trials and conflicts to be settled; his propositions would be destroyed if they were dissected into their thematic components. All they seek is a frame of modulation (that is, the shifts of key that give music its feeling of light and shade) within which they find their space, can surrender to their self-absorption. In these sonatas, at least, Schubert's hope seems undimmed.

Why did *Hausmusik* decline in popularity? Because Rossini had arrived in Vienna, sweeping everything before him. German opera was *passé*: Salieri had given up writing for the stage long ago. The censors' suspicion of disguised social comment meant that there was room only for pantomime, farces, and spectaculars to make the philistines goggle. Beethoven admitted how infectiously Italian melodies appealed to the 'frivolous sensuality' of the time.

Hedonistic froth provides the occasion to which Schubert rises in the *Sixth Symphony* (D589), his first attempt to write an ostentatious orchestral party-piece, which he began in October 1817. The ground plan is clearly Beethoven's *First*, but there's a flamboyant theatricality to which Beethoven never aspired, through which a twenty-year-old struggles to break free of his early symphonic language. It was performed by Otto Hatwig's amateur orchestra in 1818, and sank without trace.

An Italian flavour in overtures at least gave Schubert his first public performance, when either the *D major* (D590) or *C major* (D591) was played by musicians from the Theater Wien at the Hotel Der römische Kaiser in March 1818. The *Theaterzeitung* reviewed the concert:

> *The second part began with a wonderfully lovely overture by a young composer, Herr Franz Schubert, a pupil of the famous Salieri. He has learnt already how to touch and move all hearts to emotion. Although the theme is simple enough, a wealth of the most astonishing and agreeable ideas developed from it, worked out with vigour and skill. It is to be wished that this artist will quite soon delight us with another new gift.*

To Germans, Italianate style was a byword for superficiality. Schubert, always a free thinker, revelled in its racy good humour. At this stage changing styles were for him simply new costumes in which he could wrap his own unique idiosyncrasies, with no jingoistic or moral implications. The overwrought pathos of Mediterranean opera was there to be made fun of. Schubert learned from Rossini, using those lessons to powerful effect in the tragic *F minor Fantasia*, which he composed in the last year of his life. In any case, if evidence were needed of Schubert's lofty Teutonic credentials, he had already provided it in his first commission, the cantata '*Prometheus*' (D451). This he wrote for Leopold von Sonnleithner, a supporter of Schubertiads, who sang in the chorus and paid the nineteen-year-old composer forty gulden for the privilege when the music was given in the garden of Sonnleithner's Erdberggasse house on 24 July 1816. It lasted three quarters of an hour, and it impressed its listeners profoundly. Its manuscript has been lost for 150 years.

The crucial event of these years is Schubert's meeting with the man who became his provider, his advocate and mentor, alongside whom he would give the first recitals of song as an art-form. Johann Vogl was, it was said, 'an actor ascending to the pulpit': an opera singer whose intervals were spent reading Marcus Aurelius and Plato. He has been described as:

> *A huge man from whose huge mouth issued an astonishing voice, a baritone both flexible and smooth, capable of stentorian and of*

gentle tones. He was well over six feet tall, strong . . . lordly in movement, lordly in stride. Having been brought up in a Jesuit college, he never lost a tendency to self-analysis, a moral scepticism applied to himself and to the world.

Vogl had been a star at the Vienna Opera for twenty years, singing such roles as Orestes in Gluck's *Iphigenia* (where Schubert had first heard him) and Pizarro in the revised *Fidelio*. Schubert expressed an urge to meet him and Schober, endlessly hectoring a world-weary man who knew his own greatness, at last arranged an appointment at Landskrongasse in the spring of 1817. Spaun describes Vogl's appearance:

At the appointed hour he entered gravely, and the little insignificant-looking Schubert made him an awkward bow, thanked him for the great honour, and in his embarrassment stammered a few nonsensical phrases, Vogl lifted his eyebrows. A bad beginning! Vogl said, 'Well, what have you here? Accompany me,' and took a sheet of music paper lying on the piano. It contained 'Augenlied', a pretty but not especially important song. He hummed rather than sang. 'Not bad,' he said somewhat coldly. But then he looked at 'Memnon', 'Ganymed' and other songs; singing with a half-voice, he became friendlier. He departed without committing himself. Before he left he tapped Schubert on the shoulder. 'You have talent,' he said, 'but you are too little the actor, too little the charlatan. You are too prodigal with fine thoughts, without developing them.'

Schubert thought the interview a failure. But Vogl was more impressed than he cared to admit, and soon returned. The songs he had seen had not let him rest. An idea had come: he was now nearing fifty, an age that spelled the end of an operatic career. But here, with the work of this young man, a new possibility opened. He would become an interpreter of these extraordinary songs, which required not only singing but acting. 'The enthusiasm with which this magnificent artist performed' continues Spaun, 'had the greatest effect on the young composer himself, who was overjoyed to see his long-nourished hopes fulfilled beyond all his expectations.' So Schubert and Vogl set out, performing not only in the houses of educated Viennese but in nearby Austrian towns.

However, it was not some new champion who had deepened the inward meditation of his songs from the end of 1816. It was Mayrhofer and his contacts from Prague northwards, contemplating the failure of liberalism across Europe, which helped to lead Schubert from Rossini back to Mayrhofer's own poems, to Schiller, and finally the Goethe of *'Wilhelm Meister'*.

The first of these songs are strophic; and the repetition of strophes demands a refinement in harmony, a more delicate appreciation of the music that is there to be gathered behind each poet's words. The profundity Schubert now finds draws from him a harmonic boldness that (as we know from his second thoughts) sometimes frightens him.

'Gruppe aus dem Tartarus' (D396), best of the Schiller settings, has a chromaticism that still seems audacious. While travelling on a mailcoach Goethe had written *'An Schwager Kronos'*, depicting a demon-postilion on his journey through this world as a ravenous adventurer of fortune who, having tasted life to the full, determines to drive triumphantly into the night of hell. Schubert's setting (D369) is recklessly superb: a brilliant staccato figure clings to the changing metre and climbs on chromatically rising modulations, as the traveller drives hard into the mountains. With the same magnificent clarity that has guided him through life, he foresees his plunge into the abyss.

Five of Schubert's greatest songs are from March 1817, and the ink can hardly have been dry when Vogl made his entrance. The setting of Goethe's *Ganymed* (D544) summons an antique world in a hymn of rapturous sweetness; Mayrhofer's *Memnon* (D541) uses a mythological parallel of unbearable melancholy. Schober's *An die Musik* (D547) becomes Schubert's own hymn to artistic creation. Claudius's *'Der Tod und das Mädchen'* (D531) and Schubert's *'Die Forelle'* (*'The Trout'*, D550) were to achieve fame in very different guises, as we shall see.

December 1817 saw Schubert dejected and alone. At Schober's he had become a salon celebrity, but Schober's brother Axel returned from France, and needed his room. Schubert had long since said his goodbye to Therese with a keepsake book of songs, and Franz the elder would only accept him back if he became an assistant again. When Schubert's family moved to a school at Rossau, he went with them. His emotional crisis has left us only a couple of striking choruses for male voices, which are without precedent. Yet his luck was about to change, for the roots of his fame were in place.

Schubert's songs are enriched by his grasp of the operatic treatment of arias in Mozart's operas, and by his own symphonic experiments. There is no better postlude to this period in his life than a little gem of his ripening maturity, the *Fifth Symphony in B flat* (D485), which he composed between September and October 1816. If it presents a nostalgic aside after his *Fourth*, it is also a spiritual expansion of chamber music that is both intimate and great. It is the Mozart of the *Fortieth Symphony*, the violin sonatas and great piano concertos, the *G major Quartet* and *G minor Quintet*, reappraised with Schubertean poetry and rhythmic verve. As the English musicologist Donald Tovey wrote, 'a pearl of rare price'.

But that cannot be the emotional postlude, I think. In 1827, Hummel and his pupil Ferdinand Hiller came to hear one of Vogl and Schubert's last recitals, which undoubtedly contained songs from these three early years. In 1871 Hiller recalled the event:

One song followed another – the givers were tireless, the receivers were tireless. Schubert had little technique, and Vogl had little voice left, but both had such life and feeling that it would have been impossible to perform these wondrous compositions with greater clarity or with greater sincerity.

We thought neither of the playing, nor of the songs: it was as though the music had no need of any material sound, as though the melodies were revealing themselves to ethereal ears. I cannot speak of my emotions but my master, who after all had almost half a century of music behind him, was so deeply moved that the tears were trickling down his cheeks.

CHAPTER 4
THE YOUNG MASTER
(1818–22)

Early in July 1818 Schubert arrived at the castle of Zseliz on the Esterházy estate. The explanation was simple: the Count needed a piano teacher for his daughters Maria and Caroline. Schubert was cheap, available, and came with the recommendation of a mutual friend, Karl Unger.

There was a room waiting for him in the servants' outhouse:

> ... Forty geese set up such a cackling that one can hardly hear oneself speak. The people around me are all, without exception, very nice.... The cook is something of a rake, the chambermaid thirty years old, the housemaid very pretty and often my companion, the governess a good old thing, the butler my rival. The Count is rather rough; the Countess haughty but more refined; the two little girls are nice children. So far I have been spared the ordeal of dining with the family.

When Caroline reproached him for not dedicating music to her, he replied, 'What's the point? It's all dedicated to you anyway.' Inevitably piano music stands out among his works at this time: duets, German dances, military marches; all those genres that a publisher could be relied on to buy, and which our unsociable age of virtuosity-in-plastic has consigned to history. The quality of Schubert's duets is magnificent, their quantity enormous. Were they his compensation for hearing so little of his own orchestral work? Perhaps. More to the point, his genre-pieces are poems confided to the keyboard, songs freed from the demands of sonata form.

The sonatas themselves show Schubert fighting to outstrip his models. There is a turbulent fragment in F minor (D625) in which the Beethoven of the '*Appassionata*' is answered by episodes of bittersweet serenity: others too, in C major and C sharp minor. The conclusion of this first period in his *Sonatas* is the *A major* (D664), in which a glow of innocent enchantment disguises writing of enviable elegance, unity, symmetry. The slow movement's resigned happiness anticipates '*Der Unglückliche*' (D713), which Schubert wrote in 1821: the finale echoes a song already complete, '*Hänflers Liebeswerbung*' (D552). But the A major takes us ahead of ourselves, to Josefine von Koller, the events of 1819 – and to the last sonata Schubert was to write, where the elysium of D664 is tinged with awe.

His disillusionment with Zseliz came quickly. 'Here I am all alone in the depths of Hungary, without a single person with whom I can exchange an intelligent word.' And in another letter, 'My longing for Vienna grows daily.' When in November the Esterházys visited his home city, Schubert came with them and did not go back. Franz the elder wrote a petition to a high church dignitary to draw his son at last into the fold, but Schubert would have none of it and moved in with Mayrhofer. Relations between the two young men were cordial, and great settings of Mayrhofer led to greater Goethe, as if personal friendship tapped the creative springs from which Goethe could draw still finer music.

These were the circumstances in which Schubert was asked to write '*Die Zwillingsbrüder*' (D647), a *Singspiel* (a drama with speech as well as singing) lifted from Georg von Hoffmann's one-act play, as a showpiece for Vogl. It was premiered in June 1819, withdrawn after six performances, and promptly moved the management of the Theater an der Wien to commission incidental music to a three-act extravaganza, '*Die Zauberharfe*' (D644). At least that survived eight performances.

Vogl's habit was to spend his summer holiday in his native Steyr, an 'inconceivably lovely' town among rolling hills. In July 1819 Schubert accompanied him and for three months they basked in the balmy admiration of local patrons. It was one of the happiest periods in Schubert's short life. He writes roguishly to his brother Ferdinand, 'At the house where I'm lodging there are eight girls, nearly all pretty – so you see, one's kept busy.'

For the vivacious daughter of a local merchant, he wrote his D664 Sonata but for Sylvester Paumgartner, an iron-master and amateur cellist, there was a more famous gift, the *'Trout' Quintet*. It was Paumgartner's suggestion, and Schubert's first instrumental masterpiece: a set of variations for piano and strings on what was already among the best-loved of the songs from 1817, framed by four graceful movements – as Hummel's *Piano Quintet* had been. But Schubert soars above that homely exemplar to create a shining serenade, in which music-making among friends is given the stamp of exuberant greatness. As the critic Maurice Brown well says, 'The Steyr countryside was a secret collaborator in the quintet; it is even fortunate in its nickname, with its suggestion of cool, sun-flecked water.'

By September, Schubert was composing ceaselessly. Four months before, he had come across the poetry of Novalis and the Nazarenes, in which the ideas of Goethe permeate a child-like love of Christ that is both confessional and mystically individual. *'Nachthymne'* (D687) is one of the best-known settings, as are *'Das Abendrot'* (D627) with its passionate devotion and *'Litanei auf das Fest Allerseelen'*, baring the simple and intimate expression of faith to which Schubert's Romantic contemporaries aspired in vain.

Until 1821, then, the songs are preoccupied with a mythic land of rapture: a paradise lost to be animated with delicate shades of harmony. Religious elation is the starting point, soon overtaken by an evocation of a chivalrous medieval age. The final outcome of Schubert's theosophy, in fact, is neither of those things: not historical nostalgia but pantheism, the belief that God is in everything and everything is God. Its surmounting glory is *'Gott in der Natur'* (D757: August 1822) in which the visible world becomes a manifestation of the eternal, and there is a moment of rapturous expressiveness in which the limitless breadth of Schubert's tonal horizon rises like a symbol of infinity. 'The dawn is but a reflection of his garment.' But who today arranges concerts for a choir of women's voices? And so it lies in neglect.

A marginally better fate has befallen *'Nachtstück'* (D672), which depicts a minstrel facing death in a moonlit glade, and which is filled with the 'sacred fervour' of the soul. It is a meditation on a cosmic scale, a longing for death. *'Sternennächte'* shivers with the splendour of night, as does the magnificent '*Im Walde*' (D708). '*Die Götter Griechenlands*' (D677), an outpouring of exquisite and almost unbearable pathos, becomes a lament for the purity of a lost classical age that survives only in 'the fairyland of song'. '*Salve Regina*' (D676) anticipates Wagner's '*Lohengrin*' in its higher simplicity; and there is Goethe's '*Prometheus*' (D674), a great monologue of defiance whose vehemence seems also to presage an opera composer of Wagnerian stature.

Through the Esterházys Schubert met Baron von Schönstein in 1820. With his fine baritone, Schönstein became after Vogl the most celebrated interpreter of the songs during the composer's lifetime. Later he introduced them to Liszt.

By concerts and word of mouth Schubert's fame was spreading: to the Imperial courts of Vienna and Venice, and through the Fröhlich sisters to Austria's eminent dramatist Franz Grillparzer. Recitals at the Kärntnertortheater were impressive, and the Sonnleithner family's private publication of *Erlkönig* met with an overwhelming public response. Marie Wagner, a young admirer, recalled of a Vogl concert:

> *We can have absolutely no idea of the effect which Schubert's songs made at that time. For a week after this golden Thursday the whole town was talking about Schubert and his songs. People fell over each other for them, copied them all out, and soon afterwards a few books of them were published by Diabelli.*

More manuscripts passed from hand to hand. The *Theaterzeitung*, in its Goethe review of 22 May 1821, spoke of 'a glorious wreath of song' and the general belief was that Schubert stood on the threshold of a brilliant career. The Sonnleithners were so heartened that they were even able to pay his shoe-maker.

New-found confidence manifested itself in a sumptuous ripeness and refinement to the piano accompaniments for Schubert's *Lieder*. What happened was this: Goethe had turned his own attention to transfigured Persian verse in the hopes of courting Marianne Jung, a demoiselle half his age. Marianne responded with poetry as good as his, signing herself Suleika. The two lovers parted, never met again, and Goethe passed off all of their two hundred poems as his own.

Schubert seized upon them. To '*Versunken*' (D715), with its teasing intimations of love-play and falling tresses of hair, he gives a fulminating erotic charge. '*Geheimes*' ('Secrets', D719) has soft charm: the poet knows the meaning of a glance, it promises 'the next sweet hour.' Brahms called '*Suleika I*' (D720) 'the loveliest song ever written'. The throbbing agitation of the piano, with its shiver of major and minor before an exultant climax and an ending of calm acquiescence, summons the vision of incandescent hope seemingly tempered by the aching inevitability of loss. '*Suleika II*' (D717) is buoyantly happy pastoral. Its dedicatee, the soprano Anna Milder, wrote to Schubert, 'It is heavenly and always moves me to tears. It is indescribable: you have infused it with all possible magic.'

Then came the discovery of Friedrich Rückert, later to be adopted by Mahler, and Schubert's settings of '*Sei mir gegrüßt*' (D741) and '*Du bist die Ruh*' ' (D776) are among the most marvellous of songs. And there was a masterly first movement for strings: the *Quartettsatz* of December 1820 (D703), in which a poignant melody is played off against a desperate tremolando. It is without precedent and represents a gathering of new strength: it anticipates the *Eighth Symphony* in its structure and expression of feeling; but after forty bars of the second movement, a rich and tragic Andante, the music breaks off. It was never finished.

Schubert's crowning ambition, too, still eluded him. In August 1821 he began the *Symphony in E* (D729): sketched from beginning to end too thinly to be reconstructed, but sufficiently to reveal itself as a tantalizing link between the *Sixth* and Schubert's symphonic maturity. Its guiding lights are the structural clarity of Haydn, the elegance of Rossini; yet it aligns the intimacy of chamber music with the eminence of what was to be the '*Great*' *C major* (D944) in its span and its depth of sonority. In its command, too, of daring harmonic dislocations and rhythmic change, it is music which feels its way into the unknown with unerring sureness.

In March 1845, Mendelssohn wrote to Ferdinand Schubert:

I received through Doctor Haertel the symphony sketch by your brother, of which you have made me the possessor. What pleasure you give me through so fine, so precious a gift, how deeply grateful I am for this remembrance of the deceased master. Believe me that you could have given it to no one who would have had greater

*joy in it. It seems to me as if, through the very incompleteness
of the work – the scattered, half-finished intentions – I became
at once personally acquainted with your brother more clearly
and more intimately than I should have done through a finished
piece. It was as though I saw him there working in his room.*

SCHUBERT AND THE THEATRE

Vienna's infatuation with the stage goes back to the miracle plays.
By the baroque period, opera was felt to be 'a necessary spectacle',
promoted by the State as an endorsement for absolutism, the
divine right of Emperors. It became the highest ambition of any
Viennese composer, attested by the success not only of
Beethoven's '*Fidelio*' but also of '*Die Entführung aus dem Serail*' and
Mozart's '*Die Zauberflöte*' and, in 1821, Weber's triumphant '*Der
Freischütz*'.

Now, Schubert's flair for choral and theatrical writing is
evident from what he called his 'Easter cantata' of 1820, *Lazarus*.
He had been interested in the problems of combining dramatic
speech with song in such a way so as not to disturb the flow of
the music. The traditional solution drew a sharp distinction
between recitative and aria, but Schubert had already experi-
mented with the song-like treatment of speech (*arioso*) and at
last he carried the idea further, so that *Lazarus* demands to be
regarded as an opera as highly evolved as a great many from the
late-nineteenth century. Alfred Einstein comments, 'If we say
that, from the point of view of the historical development of opera
Schubert's fragment far surpasses *Tannhäuser* and *Lohengrin*, we
are not making to great a claim. [*Lazarus*] anticipates everything
that Lysiart or Telramund have to say . . . it is a perfect work of
art.' Schubert left it incomplete, but he wrote more than enough
to unmask the story of his rambling ineptitude.

What went wrong for Schubert's operas? *Die Zwillingsbrüder*
had been adapted from French farce (*Les deux Valentins*) by the
secretary of the Kärntnertor theatre, yet the management there
was in no hurry to stage the piece when it became clear that would
clash with the premiere of *Otello*. To compete with Rossini was a
daunting challenge, and Schubert could not provide what the
public had come to expect. As a native composer the single door
open to him was German operetta, unless he could strike out into
fresh ground where his contemporaries could only ape Mozart.

He pinned his hopes on a resurgence of German opera, yet the Italian impresario Domenico Barbaja was about to be given a twelve-year contract to manage the Court Opera at the Kärntner-tor itself. At Schubert's first night there was a body politic of claques, as the critic from Leipzig reported: 'That Herr Schubert has many friends who were very active in promoting him was evident at the first performance. But they may have forgotten that between fiasco and furore, as the Italians say, there is tre-mendous difference.' Needless to say that whenever supporters cheered, a rival faction hissed. Between them the composer disappeared.

Vogl was censured by the Leipzig press for playing twin brothers 'in such a way that one knew only too well it was the same actor who interpreted them.' Schubert, ahead of the times, was criticized from all quarters for his endless modulation of keys, while 'hardly any repose is to be met with in confused and supercharged instrumentation, anxiously striving after original-ity.' But the crux of the problem was more deep-seated. Schubert wrote for an audience that had abandoned Gluck, and he had never learnt the hard lessons of *opera buffa* and *opera seria*, on which his peers had cut their teeth. The *Allgemeine Musikalische Zeitung* noted:

> *Herr Schubert is too much wedded to details of the text; he tries to express words in music instead of the nature of a whole speech by means of the character of a whole piece. . . . The music has much originality and many interesting passages, but it is a blot on the work that the sentiments of simple country folk are inter-preted too seriously, not to say heavy-handedly, for a comic subject.*

Put bluntly: too many songs, too little feel for greasepaint. How-ever, it was the last time that Schubert's sense of context failed him so utterly. After seeing *Die Zauberharfe* Josef Rosenbaum wrote in his diary, 'Wretched trash, quite failed to please, the machinery gibbed and went badly, although nothing remarkable. Nobody knew his part: the prompter was always heard first.' Several Viennese reviewers made clear that that failure of this second platitude was due to the stultified tedium of its plot and dialogue. 'True, there is music – and real music! Many good ideas, forceful passages, cleverly managed harmonic pieces, insight and understanding.' Such was the *Theaterzeitung*'s evisceration of the score that had failed to overcome 'a flood of boredom'. The *Conversationblatt* added, 'What a pity that Schubert's wonderfully beautiful music has not found a worthier subject.'

It would be the same fate for *Rosamunde, Fürsten von Zypern* (D797), the doggerel play for which Schubert composed incidental music in 1823 as a favour to Leopold Kupelwieser, who was hot-foot in pursuit of an actress. It has been claimed that Schubert's taste deserted him when it came to choosing texts for the theatre, but not so. He needed a stage success to secure his reputation, and he made the best of what he could get: the trite Viennese sentimentality of Kotzebue and his lame literary imitators. An *A flat Mass* (D678), which Schubert hoped would win fame and favours from the Imperial Court where his operas had failed, draws on its established texts to create a work of major stature. But it was too personal, too difficult and subjective, to make headway.

In September 1821, Schubert and Schober left for the castle of Ochsenburg at St Pölten in order to complete another opera: *Alfonso und Estrella*, a tale of love at first sight set within two opposing noble families ((D732). The libretto is another cobbled pastiche. All hopes and rumours foundered, for Barbaja turned it down. Weber, impressed by what Schober had called 'the rich and teeming ideas' of Schubert's score, promised to produce the work in Berlin. It did not come to pass, and with Vogl temporarily estranged, there was nobody else to speak on Schubert's behalf. By the end of 1823 and *Fierabras*, his disillusionment with the theatrical world was complete.

'They put on rubbish' he wrote to Anselm Hüttenbrenner, 'which makes one's hair stand on end.' Or in exhaustion to Spaun, 'I should be quite well if this wretched business of the opera were not so mortifying.' In the wake of *Die Zauberharfe* there is a contemptuous poem, *Der Geist der Welt*, where Schubert attacks 'those who with wrangling fill these days.'

His friends, too, were going: Mayrhofer left Vienna, Therese Grob had married a master baker, and when Spaun was transferred to Linz as a tax-inspector, Schubert composed a verse, '*Und nimmer schreibst du?*' ('And never do you write'). Spaun suggested he set it to music, but the result ('*Herrn Josef Spaun, Assessor in Linz*', D749) is not the carefree parody of an Italian recitative and aria that its recipient took it to be. It is the shriek of a man who, in 1822, begins to perceive that his life is in ruins.

The story does not end there. In 1867, Sir Arthur Sullivan and Sir George Grove found the music to *Rosamunde* in what Grove recalled as 'a bundle of music books two feet high, and black with the dust of decades. These were the part books of the whole of the music in *Rosamunde*, tied up after the second performance in December 1823, and probably never disturbed since.'

Tense with excitement at what Grove called this 'treasure', the eminent Victorians copied scores until two in the morning. Then, in the night air, they played a game of leapfrog.

CHAPTER 5

ILLNESS AND TRAUMA
(1822–23)

♦ *Schubert's seduction*
♦ *. . . and the aftermath*

The six little *Moments Musicaux* (D780), of which the earliest come from 1823, are among the most experimental and intimately lovely of Schubert's piano works: the most sociable and yet the most enigmatic. They are worlds within grains of sand, each detail making sense within itself.

The last of them, in A flat, is worthy to stand as the minuet to an unwritten sonata; but Edward T. Cone has noted disquiet beneath its self-possessed appearance, where promissory gestures are overwhelmed in an increasingly futile struggle. A parasitic vice appears within the harmonies of this music: at first as a novelty, then as a dangerous alternative, and lastly as a poison. All that survives its attack is the shell.

From now on, as Cone put it, 'a cold wind seems to blow through even Schubert's sunniest music.' It is haunted by the ghost – the dread – of something else. He quotes Edmund Wilson's essay on the fiction of Oscar Wilde:

> *Tragic heroes are shown in the peculiar position of suffering from organic maladies without, up to a point, being forced to experience the evils entailed by them. . . . But in the end, the horror breaks out: the afflicted one must recognize himself and be recognized by other people as the odious creature he is, whose disease or disability will kill him.*

Wilde knew that he was suffering from syphilis.

Having rejected the devotion of the 'cherubic' artist Moritz von Schwind, with whom he had been living, Schubert moved in among the Persian drapes and dressing gowns of the flat in which Schober frittered away his mother's fortune, and soon his guest's earnings. This was in 1822. He had dedicated his seductive '*Geheimes*' to Schober; and in a letter he wrote, 'Only you, dear Schober, I shall never forget, for what you meant to me no one else can mean, alas!' Schober was the cause of the current rift between Schubert and Vogl, reported by Anselm Hüttenbrenner:

> *To me Vogl is extremely pleasing. He told me all about his relationship to Schubert with the utmost frankness, and unfortunately I am quite unable to excuse the latter. Vogl is very much embittered against Schober, for whose sake Schubert behaved most ungratefully towards Vogl....*

It may be fortuitous that Vogl (a fop and 'odd old bachelor', declared Edward von Bauernfeld), was known to Schubert's coterie as 'the Greek bird', and that in Classical Greece the gift of an adult game bird to a youth was evidence of amorous intent. Nevertheless, approached in 1858 for a Schubert biography, Joseph Kenner writes of a friendship he had broken off in 1816:

> *Schubert's genius subsequently attracted, among other friends, the heart of a seductively amiable and brilliant young man ... whose scintillating individuality, as I was told later, won a lasting and pernicious effect over Schubert's honest sensibility.... This intimation seemed to me indispensible to a biographer's grasp of the subject, for it concerns an episode in Schubert's life which only too probably caused his premature death and certainly hastened it.*

Days later he is more explicit:

> *By Schubert's seducer I meant Franz von Schober. Under the guise of ... engaging affection, there reigned in this whole family a deep moral depravity, so that it was not to be wondered that Franz von Schober went the same way. The need for love and friendship emerged with such egotism and jealousy ... he was willing to tolerate no other religion, no morals, no restraint.*

At this time, Schubert joined a clandestine club of young men – actors, writers, opera-singers – meeting upstairs near the Kärntnertor under the guidance of their leading light Ignaz Castelli, whom they called 'the Calif'. After drinking past midnight, there were pranks to play: pulling the doorbells of sleeping neighbours and running off.

The police became interested; and perhaps there was something else besides, for as his friend Bauenfeld confided to a diary in 1826, 'Schubert is ailing. He needs "young peacocks" like Benvenuto Cellini.' Cellini, of course, had stood accused as 'a dirty sodomite'. A peacock – in language current since the Renaissance – was a transvestite rent-boy.

What happened in 1822 will never be known.

By the end of February 1823, Schubert was housebound with his family in the Rossau, and in May he became a patient at Vienna's General Hospital, for mercury treatment. The symptoms were those of secondary syphilis: nausea, giddiness, rashes, anaemia, loss of hair, inflammation of the glands, and crippling headaches.

In his poem *A Prayer*, he contemplated suicide:

> . . . *See, abased in dust and mire*
> *Scorched by agonising fire,*
> *I in torture go my way*
> *Nearing doom's destructive day.*
>
> *Take my life, my flesh and blood*
> *Plunge it all in Lethe's flood*
> *To a stronger, purer state*
> *Deign me, Great One, to translate.*

By summer, his remission was sufficient for Schubert to join Vogl at Steyr, but he was aware he was living out the remains of a life-sentence. To the end he was unable to control his appetite, whilst knowing full well its consequences.

In 1825, Schwind urged him to conceal 'fleshly and spiritual needs – or rather your need for pheasants and punch' if he hoped to obtain the post of Court Organist, adding: 'We shall have to play on our own pipes.'

A year earlier, Schubert had written to Kupelwieser:

Imagine a man whose health will never be right again and who, in his despair over this, constantly makes things worse instead of better; imagine a man, I say, whose brightest hopes have come to nothing, to whom the joy of love and friendship offer nothing but pain, whose enthusiasm for beauty threatens to vanish; and then ask yourself if he is not indeed a wretched unhappy creature? 'My peace is gone, my heart is heavy, I shall never find it, nevermore.' Thus indeed I can sing every day, for each night, when I go to sleep, I hope I shall not wake again, and each morning reminds me only of yesterday's grief.

With zeal he undertook the three hundred works of his last four summers. Music became his redemption, and he wrote most fluently when most depressed, without a trace of self-pity.

Getting to grips with the significance of one artist's truth to himself is the purpose of the rest of this book.

CHAPTER 6

THE 'UNFINISHED' SYMPHONY AND FIRST SONG CYCLE (1822–23)

- ♦ The 'Wanderer' Fantasy
- ♦ The 'Unfinished' Symphony
- ♦ Die schöne Müllerin

The last piece Schubert wrote before his sickness was the *'Wanderer' Fantasy* (D760) of November 1822. It is the first of his mature piano works, and is dedicated to a rich amateur pianist Emmanuel von Liebenburg. Diabelli lost no time in publishing the piece, for it appeared three months later.

The Fantasy takes its name from its main theme, which comes from the middle section of an 1816 song, *'Der Wanderer'* (D489). Throughout his life, Schubert was intrigued by the challenge of unifying a long, continuous work of several movements, and in the *Fantasy* he tackles it by adapting the same music for an opening Allegro, a solemnly expressive Adagio in which the full melodic line of the song makes its entrance, a Scherzo and a fugal Finale.

The notion of the wanderer had particular meaning to the early Romantics. He is more than a vagabond, certainly; an emblem of freedom, and also of restless alienation: a free spirit, both eager and wistfully pensive, who finds his aim and purpose in his travels through nature. Loneliness had not acquired the menace its mention brings to modern urban man. The wanderer's outlook was that of *'Der Einsame'* (D800), with its sense of proud – almost defiant – fortitude. Seldom, then, do musical challenges and philosophical resonances coincide as fruitfully as in this C major fantasia. 'In its lyricism,' said Tovey, 'it harks back to Bach, and in its remote key relationships it looks forward to Wagner.'

Schubert takes the virtuoso glitter of Hummel and gives it exhilarated wit and momentum. The focussed thinking and command of theatre, which vanished from the operas, are crisp in every bar, through devices that only a piano can encompass: the piano's voicing and range of colour, its unique contrasts and variegations of texture, its means of achieving a sense of climax, tension and pace, its percussive athleticism and – in the closing Allegro of the *Wanderer* – sheer power.

In this one piece, Schubert set an agenda for the bravura keyboard showpieces of the high Romantic period. Liszt admired the *Wanderer* and made a well-meaning transcription for piano and orchestra; but his lasting acknowledgement is his own *B minor Sonata*, which takes through-composition (that is, musical structure as a seamless development) a step further. Schumann revered it, and the *Wanderer* has as much claim as Beethoven's late sonatas to be seen as inspiration for the great *C major Fantasia* of 1838. But it has also denied us greater music, for (doubtless scenting ready money) Schubert set aside the Scherzo of his *Eighth Symphony* (D759) to write it. When the time came to return, the symphony was associated with events he found repellent, and it was never completed.

What is there left to say about the world's best-loved orchestral music? The *'Unfinished'* *Symphony* stands the world of the *'Trout'* on its head. Joy has turned to disappointment through which the presence of genius burns in its poetry and compassion. Three movements were sketched in piano score, and two orchestrated, during October 1822. It was abandoned, found its way to Anselm Hüttenbrenner, and had its first performance in Vienna in 1865. Nothing else is known of its origins or fate, but decades of rumours of an unknown stroke of genius were confirmed.

As Paul Henry Lang wrote, the *'Unfinished'* is 'a work whose every tone is Schubert's own, and which can be placed next to those of Beethoven without paling. Never in the subsequent history of music did this happen again.' It is a miracle in organization and economy within a sense of arched space, in emotional intensity and poise. Not a note could be added or taken away. It has the command of a master who knows he will be understood, who can dare without taking risks, who can say what had previously taken pages within the measure of one bar. Its Allegro moderato is a superbly integrated sonata movement of extraordinary tension, in the faraway key of B minor, the source of songs for Schubert filled with an unearthly, magnetic charge.

Such preternatural grace is, as Einstein says, 'fathomless; and the expression of poignant melancholy, the outbursts of despair, could be answered only by the innocence of the *Ländler*-like second subject' for cellos. The symphony's second movement, simple in form, 'needs no melodic development, only the interplay of small or large melodic groups of magical charm and magical euphony.' Did Schubert realize that nothing more could match it, or feel that he had simply said enough? At any rate, material from a projected finale may survive as the B minor Entr'acte in '*Rosamunde*'.

Syphilis, like the prospect of hanging, does wonders to concentrate the mind. Such adventures as the *Wanderer* seemed suddenly out of the question. Schubert's first mature sonata is contemporary with his suicidal poetry: the A minor of February 1823 (D784), where lyricism is renounced in favour of pianism on an orchestral scale.

Not that there is any trace of the *Wanderer*'s exhibitionism in this tersely tragic work, whose monumentality and dramatic violence unfold on purely instrumental terms. We are offered a darkening underworld, a place of plunging silences and sinister whispers, above which the apparition of lost bliss hovers like a phantasm. Heard after the fearful marches of an *Allegro giusto* (did Bruckner in his *Eighth Symphony*, or Mahler – ever – say more than Schubert could in fourteen minutes?), the monothematic Andante has the quality of one of those flowers that open only in the night, and which might be visited by Fuseli's night-creatures. If the last movement of Chopin's '*Funeral March*' *Sonata* can be described as 'gossip' then so, in desolation, is the finale here; more even than '*An Schwager Kronos*', it is music from an abyss. It is a landmark that precedes the cosy Romanticism of Mendelssohn's midsummer night and outstrips it by fifty years.

Convalescence meant being cut off from society, like a leper. As Beethoven's nephew Karl remarks in their conversation book, 'Everyone speaks very highly of Schubert, but they say he has gone into hiding.' To pay his hospital bills he was forced into rash business deals. First he sold for a negligible lump sum his publi-

cation rights to a corpus of work. This was again to Cappi &
Diabelli, with whom he instantly broke off dealings when he
suspected them of sharp practice. His next publishers, Sauer and
Leindesdorf, were incompetent to the point of bankruptcy –
which forced him cap-in-hand back to his original arrangements.
Schubert's friends looked on in dismay; but unlike Beethoven he
had no patrons, none of Hummel's or Salieri's favour in high
places. Again he took what he could, but in financial matters (as
in his personal welfare) he was prone to self-neglect.

Solace came in an outpouring of songs. In December 1822,
he had composed '*Nachtviolen*' (D752), a marvel of cryptic intimacy, luscious and delicate and supremely simple, whose significance is deeper than its surface meaning – as we shall see. There
had been the '*Der Musensohn*' (D764), which dances off through
clear air to a land of immortal youth, and early in 1823 '*Du Bist die
Ruh*' ' (D776) a devotional and almost transcendent suggestion
of a satisfied lover's peace. Collin's '*Der Zwerg*' (D771) is the story
of a court dwarf who strangles on board a boat the queen with
whom he is infatuated. Schubert, laughing, set it in a few minutes
flat – and transmutes something faded and grotesque into music
whose fatalistic gloom chills the heart.

But the prize of 1823 is '*Auf dem Waßer zu Singen*' (D774),
which depicts the soul departing upon water in the evening
sunlight. It is the supreme evocation of *Sehnsucht* : the early
Romantics' longing for a mystic world of the spirit, with our
temporal world as mere shimmering appearance. There is no
greater instance of the haunted ambivalence that underlies all
Schubert's work than this fluttering juxtaposition of major and
minor, of longing and radiant fulfilment, capturing at the same
moment fervour and rapturous serenity.

FIRST SONG CYCLE

The origins of the story about a beautiful maid of the mill, one of
whose suitors kills himself, are difficult to trace. It was the subject
of Paisiello's opera *L' amor contrastato* (1788), which made a triumphant progress through Germany under the title '*Die schöne
Müllerin*'. But Goethe had also written a sequence on the subject
of a young man who loses his heart to a miller's daughter, and
there is a whole section in '*Des Knaben Wunderhorn*', the famous
anthology of folk-poetry. Paisiello was the toast of Berlin after the

Napoleonic Wars; and, adapted as a party-game, his plot was picked up by Wilhelm Müller, a young Romantic whose best poetry celebrated the Greek struggle for liberty, but who himself had plenty of experience of unrequited love. Müller was nagged by his circle of friends to write out his extemporized contributions, which appeared in newspapers and which, as *Seventy-seven Poems from the Posthumous Papers of a Travelling Horn-player*, were published in full during 1821.

How Schubert came across them is not clear. The story is that he pocketed them from Benedikt Randhartinger's library and presented the astonished owner with his settings next morning. More likely he had been introduced to them by Weber in 1822. However it happened, in Schubert's hands they became the vehicle for one of the great leaps forward in musical possibility, which kept him busy both in and out of hospital during 1823. Selecting twenty-six of the poems, he presents us with a journey of one man's discovery: beginning with homespun images of masculinity in the open air, then the fantasy of virility, of being desired and of absolute, infatuated possession (the miller's daughter is a *tabula rasa* upon which the wandering hired hand projects his self-belief), continuing through jealousy and doubt into the realization of devastating failure.

Seven years earlier, Beethoven had published his own song-sequence on the subject of love, *An die ferne Geliebte*. Schubert knew it, and ignored it. He created instead an evolving drama with an underlying thread: recognizing that the poetry had been written under the influence of Goethe, and digging into the scenic and dramatic resources he had himself developed in setting Goethe's work. He was stirred by the notion of overwhelming emotions mirrored in nature; and if Müller's verses are naive, Schubert's treatment has the sophisticated subterfuge of artlessness, fashioning something that feels as natural as folksong. He had come to terms with Schiller's allegories, he knew the language he was looking for, the tensions and resolutions he could exploit: its iconography too, the imagery of the young Romantic world. He took the language of flowers and dragged it towards the language of Tristan, summoning a universality and force that poems alone could not approach.

He creates an archetype, a myth at a new pitch of expressiveness; a variety yet cumulative wholeness which adds a new dimension of sustained drama and narrative to the song form.

Romanticism brought fresh intensity to language, but German poetry has always had Arcadian leanings. Goethe is not the intellectual in his love-poems that Shakespeare or Dante are, but someone close to nature. Schubert, above all, lacks guile: he is never courtly, never sopisticated. As Richard 'Capell said of a composer whose outlook often seems too trusting to have known disillusionment:

> *He roams at will. Schubert's* Arcadia *is his whole known world, from which he never conceives of an escape. There is no bitterness . . . for Schubert has everything to find out for himself. That is why we cannot help thinking of him as a shepherd, fluting away his young days in grassy solitude.*

Not quite, for the leitmotiv of his music is the sound of flowing water, which stands for life. The suggestion of a stream runs through '*Die schöne Müllerin*', whether overtly or as some hidden presence, and the waves seem to adumbrate the moods with astonishing psychological aptness, and become their commentary. Only in excesses of the travelling miller's imagination does the stream disappear: it is his source of counsel, the fountain of innocence and vitality from which he tries to break free, and in the end, the coldness that drowns him. Charles Rosen writes of the connexion between an awareness of landscape and the awareness of death:

> *The most signal triumphs of the Romantic portrayal of memory are not those that recall past happiness, but remembrances of those moments when future happiness still seemed possible. There is no greater pain than to remember past happiness in a time of grief – but that is the classical tradition of the tragedy of memory. Romantic memories are often those of absence, of that which never was.*

In these circumstances the fragrance of a flower, an ill-wind, a sound from the past, even '*die böse Farbe*', an evil colour, brings with it a spectre taken out of place and time. As Rosen continues, 'These memories do not cause the past to live again; they make us feel its death.' Such emblems, to the Romantics, are more than literary conceits, more than convenient ellipsis. They are a totem as much alive as sinews and bone.

Schubert intensifies Müller by stripping him of dramatic events, even of anecdote. We are left with the trivialities of everyday life (a discarded ribbon, the glimpse of a reed flute) whose significance becomes that of life or death. For the first time in his music, Schubert gives us a purely lyrical expression that moves towards the inevitability of physical extinction – just as *Winterreise*, four years later, would take the same persona (older, wiser, embittered) to show it suffer spiritual death.

It is impossible to separate these songs from their ordered place, because each establishes the emotional atmosphere for the next. Schubert opens with pastoral music: the miller's carefree vigour, the swing of the mill-wheels and muscles of steel are caught in the same flourish. The cycle's emotional climax, '*Mein!*' is followed by the ambiguous hush of '*Pause*', after which anything might happen. '*Die liebe Farbe*' ('the beloved colour') is a quiet crescendo of heartbreak, falling apart at the tempo of a pulse, using the tonality of alienation and derangement. It has a numbness that lies beyond jealousy and despair, an uncomprehending obsession that anticipates suicide. Yet the end, when it comes, is handled with the delicacy of a lullaby.

Schubert's control depends on the finesse of his tonal progressions, which cater for every opposition and nuance of tone and meaning. Briefly, '*Der Müller und der Bach*' uses a language that clashes as violently as any discord in Liszt's tempestuous *Vallée d'Obermann*. More often, the listener must remember earlier songs in the cycle to make sense of fleeting harmonic subtleties. The pivotal piece is '*Thränenregen*' ('shower of tears'), in which the first intimation of failure is palpable: and we realize that '*Mein!*', which follows it, is phrased in the past tense. It is the recollection of what never was.

How far away the certainties of the classical world have receded. Rosen concludes, 'The song cycle is the most original musical form created in the first half of the nineteenth century. It most clearly embodies the Romantic conception of experience as a gradual unfolding and illumination.' The form of Schubert's song cycle is no less precise than that of a classical sonata, but its precision is only gradually comprehended as it unfolds. This is the lesson Schubert now brings to his instrumental music.

CHAPTER 7
SCHUBERT'S HIGH SUMMER
(1824–27)

♦ Four piano sonatas
♦ The great chamber music
♦ The last symphony
♦ Schubert the song-writer

Posterity's problem in grasping the reasons why Schubert writes as he does owes a little to his status as a transitional figure between Classicism and the Romantics. It has far more to do with an idiom that is unique to itself.

How true is it that, in assembling his larger musical structures, Schubert fails by the standards of his predecessors, as an architect of classical rigour? He has, after all, been called 'degenerate'. More to the point, how much are human emotions a rigorous thing – beyond one historical period in western man's attempts to make any sense of them?

Schubert was never happy with conventional sonata form. In his earliest pieces he grapples with it like a good student: later, it seems to bore him. And it doesn't matter, because the emotional flux of song-writing (the turbulence of a changing persona which, over the course of a song, a story-teller is able to reveal) gives him a pretext to break free from the formal straitjacket of his times. But as the critic Martin Chusid has shown, an impatience with the orthodox tensions of classical structure tingles within him from his first steps in instrumental composing.

What is classical structure? It is about contrast, and a richness of allusion that stems from the relationship of parts to the whole: an antagonism between themes which is at last resolved. But Schubert is a melodist, whose melodies are shot through with dazzling harmonic colour: that is to say, an awareness of the relationships between keys that gives known material new insight and reverberation, the changing context that enables a singing line to soar like a bird. What can he do?

Schubert's piano sonatas are both formal and informal. Formal, because his mature essays (unlike Beethoven's) have the same number of movements as a symphony: they are Schubert in his Sunday best, giving domestic music the status of a symphony. Informal, because Schubert writes away from the piano, and he wants his sonatas to have the apparent spontaneity of an improvization. The slow movement of the D959 *A major Sonata* is a case in point. He begins with a barcarolle, which he needs to bring back with even greater pathos so as to draw the *Andantino* to a close. A contrast is needed, a middle section. But what a display Schubert provides! It is a storm as real as any in the '*Années de Pèlerinage*' two decades later, yet it is in a different realm: a storm of the spirit. It is a calculated attack not only on conventional form, but on the boundaries of sense itself.

When I say that Schubert is bored, I mean he seems unable to suffer any length of time in a given key without the sort of harmonic digression that is apt to burst like a firework; and his tonal iridescence cries out for a recognition unburdened by the proprieties of classical style. Already we have touched on the interplay between major and minor in Schubert's songs, and it is the conjunction between the two that gives his instrumental and orchestral work its dramatic propulsion. The opening Allegro of the D887 *Quartet* (June 1826) is torn by such violent collisions of tonality, such audacious harmonic schemes, that the choice of G major as home key seems almost fortuitous. The smallest changes find energy to drive a whole movement. Only in his last music is this post-Classical harmony most miraculously evolved; but the non-vocal works of 1824–27 see Schubert's scheme of things being worked out. Through them one can witness the tragedy in a teacup of the *Fourth Symphony* – the almost unrelieved charm of early sonatas – being supplanted by something more flexible, subtle, diverse.

For a moment we need to step forward to the piano music of his last months, including the *Piano Sonata in C minor*, D958, which is one of the most formal and one of the most questioning – the most subversive – pieces he ever wrote. Consider the first movement. Ostensibly its guiding spirit is the '*Pathétique*', and Beethoven would have been the first to relish the sound it made: mighty amplitude and emotion pared back to the cutting edge, or what Beethoven used to call 'the voice from the vault'. Its crucial tonal intervals are those of the fifth and minor sixth: expressed in different keys, but above all in a little figure of 'G – A flat – G' which serves as a pivot, a point of reference as it emerges in different guises: sometimes in the treble, sometimes in the bass, but always differently harmonized so as to suggest (in minor keys) darkness and stress; or (in the major), tension and ambiguity.

So much for the opening theme, the first subject. As it dies away in vehemence the little figure repeats more expressively, and in the second subject (a hymn-like tune of soothing warmth) its harmonization is innocently simple. This, and an echo which is shifted down a tone, means that the hymn sounds warmer still on its return, borne on a tranquil figuration in the bass.

Not for long. A dancelike variation plunges the second subject into the minor, and at the end of it, the 'G – A flat – G' motif becomes a cry of despair. To end his exposition in a mood of proper reconciliation, Schubert's harmonies return to the major, tinged with an edge of sorrow; so that the three notes sound more equivocal than before, and at last the plangency of the minor sixth is made to reveal its true identity. The music's credentials seem flawless, so far.

Soon something is not right. The development section's aggressive jostle of keys is a deliberate act of disorientation, and the coda's reprise of this material means that we end the movement not in synthesis, but in disquiet. So much for the psychology of classical form. But what is more interesting is the first movement's use of silence: the pauses in which a listener's fears intensify, to be confirmed or confounded. Here, as in the Scherzo's broken and self-interrogatory phrases, Schubert creates a climate of emotional didacticism: as if he wanted to establish a sounding-board for a state of being, for what it might be like to occupy a certain moral condition.

What, then, can be said of the slow movement's changing masks? Its subjects tackle each other as if they were voices in an evolving narrative. Such events lie a world away from the ceremonial contrasts of classicism's striving for perfection – the *ne plus ultra*: the variations of Beethoven or Mozart, which achieve transcendence when other creative options have been exhausted.

Schubert's fascination lies not with structural but with emotional potential. His music moves like a dialogue conducted in shifting light. This is what Alfred Brendel meant when he spoke of somnambulism:

> *In his larger forms, Schubert is a wanderer. He likes to move at the edge of the precipice, and does so with the assurance of a sleepwalker. To wander is the Romantic condition; one yields to it enraptured (as in the finale of the* A major Sonata) *or driven and plagued by the terror of finding no escape (as in the* C minor). *More often than not, happiness is but the surface of despair. Suddenly, the mind is overcast. Nothing is more typical of Schubert than these febrile afflictions of unease and horror.*

The falsehood of imagined order has been lost. Schubert's chaos is not that of incompetence, any more than the joy with which he revolves those moments in which he was free from care. His purpose in each is to establish not a framework but a fate. Aaron Copland described best the conception of art that strikes home for us today, and it is not the Enlightenment's:

> *Each work brings with it an element of self-discovery. I must create in order to know myself, and since self-knowledge is a never-ending search, each new work brings only a part answer to the question, 'Who am I?' and brings with it the need to go on to other and different part-answers.*

How does any work of art operate? James Joyce spoke of 'epiphanic moments' – the instance of revelation where all anticipation is suddenly transformed. Its equivalent, in music, is the *Gestalt*: a creative manipulation of the *double entrendre*, using all the devices at a composer's disposal. When it comes to manipulating his listeners' expectations, leading them on through a movement only to sweep all their preconceptions aside as deftly as a magician, Schubert is second-to-none.

I do not mean only the interlude in *'Das Lied in Grünen'* (D917), heavenly though it is. I mean something as important as the conviction held by Heidegger that poets are in the vanguard of a changed conception of being. Take the opening of the last piano sonata Schubert wrote: an endless stream of lyricism, with only three chords to hint at suspense to come. He draws back from these intimations of drama, then seizes them to press forward, changing to the minor and bringing back his glorious opening tune in a veil of ambivalence, so that it sounds more heart-breaking than ever. His 'draughtsmanship' in these bars, as Tovey lovingly called it, is one of the greatest miracles in music.

Revolutions, including Beethovenian ones, are a rattling good idea in their place: but the crackle of cordite is not the only way in which Romanticism needs to manifest itself; and if Beethoven (conspicuously in the dusty battles of his middle period, the time he wrote the '*Waldstein*' and '*Appassionata*') presents us with a robust Hegelian dialectic, we should also find time for more reflective processes of evolution. The master himself was reported to have said of Schubert, 'This one will surpass me.' So announced the Vienna newspapers in 1819; and whilst rumours are generally groundless, one suspects Beethoven might have been the first to appreciate that, if we confine music within the limits of some implacable dogma and stringency, we deny it space to grow.

The year 1824–25 was a golden one for Schubert. Beginning in despair, it ended with new friends, fame at the Musikverein, and new intellectual horizons as the craving to write a 'grand symphony' possessed his imagination. March 1824 was the occasion of his drunken tirade against two opera house musicians who were tactless enough to approach him for a commission:

> *Artists? Musical hacks is what you are, nothing else! How can anyone spend his whole life doing nothing but bite on a piece of wood with holes in it? I am an artist, I! I am Franz Schubert, whom everybody knows and recognizes. Who has written great things and beautiful things that you don't begin to understand. And who is going to write still more beautiful things: cantatas and quartets, operas and symphonies! Because I am not just a composer of* Ländler *as the stupid newspapers say and stupid people repeat – I am Schubert! And don't you forget it! You crawling, gnawing worms that ought to be crushed under my foot – the foot of the man who is reaching to the stars. To the stars,*

> *I say, whilst you poor puffing worms wriggle in the dust and*
> *with the dust are scattered and rot!*

This is Schubert on the brink of his last period, more than ever intent upon winning – as he knew he had to win – his public. He wanted to become an instrumental and orchestral composer, he declared: using the piano sonata and the string quartet as stepping stones. Death was an inevitability; meanwhile you hoped and lived. There were charades to play in convivial company, good mountain air to breathe, tours with Vogl. Yet Schwind writes of a new seriousness: 'Schubert is inhumanly busy. A new quartet is to be performed at Schuppanzigh's. . . . He has long been at work on an octet, with the greatest zeal. If you go to see him during the day he says, 'Hullo, how are you? – Good.' . . . and goes on working, whereupon you depart.

The work that was absorbing his energies, the *Octet* for strings and wind instruments (D803), was commissioned by Ferdinand Count Troyer, an amateur clarinettist, and at Troyer's suggestion modelled on Beethoven's *Septet*, Opus 20. The number of movements is the same (six), but Schubert adds a second violin, bubbling vitality and brilliance of tone. The wind are offered every chance to show their expressive *cantabile*, strikingly so in a series of enchanted dialogues. This is the '*Trout*' of a man who has known wisdom and decay: its Scherzo a joyful chase through sunshine and open country: the Minuet and Trio dancing with the easy rhythm of the *Ländler*, yet using harmonic adventures to twist euphony into artistic significance. The Theme and Variations pick up a jaunty love-duet from the early '*Die Fremde von Salamanka*'.

There is, you might say, a worm in the heart of this rose. The tremulous opening of its finale quotes Schiller's '*Schöne Welt, wo bist du?*', which, to Schubert has become associated with violated and irrecoverable joy. Yet its purpose is to make the following Allegro shine more brightly, and its brief return is an impressive dramatic stroke. The Octet is the old Divertimento – courtly, suave and sociable – infused occasionally with a new sense of a romantic quest.

The first violinist in the Octet, Ignaz Schuppanzigh, served as an occasional elder mentor to Schubert: and it was Beethoven's personal quartet (Schuppanzigh, Holz, Weiss and Linke) which gave the first performance of the *Quartet in A minor*, D804, on 14 March 1824. 'Rather slowly' felt the composer, 'but with great purity and tenderness'. The kernel of this pellucid music is its Minuet, which quotes '*Die Götter Griechenlands*': as the Octet did ('Lovely world, where are you? Return once more, fair and flowered age of nature!') but in a context of infinite sorrow: levitated beyond languor or pity into a memorial realm through two bars of stark harmony (a hushed figuration of three notes) and bare rhythm. The effect is to isolate the movement and raise it into music with the sense of a visitation, a moment of ordained time. The slow movement draws on the theme from the third Entr'acte to *Rosamunde*, which is used again in the D935 *Impromptus*, but never aches more than here. In the Hungarian finale the mood changes, within some eerie envelope, from geniality to catastrophic anguish.

Both the *A minor Quartet* and its successor in *D minor* (D810, also March 1824) were planned for inclusion in Schubert's Opus 29, and each borrows themes from his most introspective songs. The music of the D810 Scherzo is taken from the sixth of twelve tiny *German Dances* (D790) but the slow movement, *Andante con moto*, is a series of variations drawn from his song '*Der Tod und das Mädchen*'. Death here has the status it had to Mozart: 'the truest and best friend of man.' It no longer holds terror, it is an inevitability and a consolation; but neither can there be the triumphant conclusion of Beethoven's *Quartet*, Opus 95, which was written at roughly the same time. Schubert's hammering rhythm becomes a savage threat in the first movement, a funereal trudge in the second, a dance in the third and, in the finale, a variation of the Presto's momentous and deathly Tarantella. There is no question but that Schubert intended this unity, and pursued it through every bar. The stylistic gropings of the *Quartettsatz* (D703) have become a conviction of means and goals, both of which are without precedent.

The D810 *Quartet* was met (reports Franz Lachner) 'with by no means unanimous approval' by its private audience in Vienna. The same fate befell the last of this autumnal triptych, and the last quartet Schubert wrote: the *G major* (D887), which was written within ten days some two years later. Nobody, it was said, could conceive what Schubert might be driving at; and even in 1850, D887 was felt to be too demanding and uncompromising for general circulation. Its first movement is music of visionary intensity, spun on by electric collisions within the tightest constraints; yet pervaded too by the chill of Weber's opera *Der Freischütz*. The effect is of questions and answers: a sinister interchange whose significance lies outside itself. The slow movement is a lament that manages to be trenchant and menacing, and establishes an atmosphere in which any subsequent hint of optimism can be seen as no more than empty posturing.

It seems banal to mention the virtuosity with which Schubert has mastered sonata form. The *G major* lives in the same season as *Winterreise*, and it is no surprise that material of its Andante reappears there in '*Einsamkeit*'.

Between the *D minor* and *G major*, Schubert had been busy. In 1825 he made a five-month tour of Upper Austria with Vogl. It was the longest and the most productive holiday of his life. 'I find my compositions everywhere' he wrote to his father. There were new sonatas to play, new songs to sing. When he stayed with Spaun's relations in Linz, Anton Ottenwald was surprised to see him looking so well and strong, 'so comfortably bright and genially communicative'.

'I have never seen him like this' his host continues. 'Serious, profound, and as though inspired. How he talked of art, of poetry, of his youth, of the relationship of ideals to life, and so on. I was more and more amazed at such a mind.' And then Ottenwald reveals, 'By the way, he began a symphony at Gmunden, which is to be performed in Vienna this winter.' At last Schubert was within reach of his lifelong wish.

Long before Schubert's birth, the symphony had outgrown its humble origins and become the supreme vehicle for serving what was called 'the new sonata style'. The orchestra's increasing powers of projection, its self-sufficiency and penetrating sonority made it ideal to project a purely musical argument – without recourse to either a verbal text or the concerto principle of the baroque era. Demanding a musical idiom that had the resources to sustain itself, the orchestra turned composers towards planning on a large (eventually a gargantuan) canvas. Instrumentation, harmonic planning, tonal structure and the deployment of themes: these were the nuts and bolts of symphonic writing, and the epitome of classical style.

As an exercise in vision, scope and integration, the possibilities of the symphony seemed limitless, and it came to be seen as no less than a challenge of the human spirit. In ground-breaking strides, it became the yardstick of greatness against which Schubert had to measure himself. He pursued it like the Holy Grail. It was, as he once said to the publisher Schott, 'the highest form of musical art'. In 1823 he had had a trail of failures and fragments behind him: now, with such indomitable music under his belt, he felt ready to tackle his mission.

For decades, the 1825 symphony was thought to be lost. We know now that it is the same as the 'Great' C major Symphony: D944, which the composer revised in the last years of his life, or appended with a fresh date in order to make it easier to sell.

Gmunden, in which he and Vogl had stayed six weeks, rests idyllically on the shores of Lake Traun. From there, the two moved on to Gastein, a spa town among mountain waterfalls. The 'Great' C major, too, is an irresistible torrent of sound. It is, as Sir Thomas Beecham was the first to say, the symphony in which Schubert proves himself to be the peer of Beethoven. It is the last great classical symphony: looking back the roots of its tradition, rediscovering Mozart's enjoyment of sheer movement, emulating the scale of Beethoven's 'Eroica' and Ninth Symphonies – and owing next-to-nothing to any of them.

Years later, Robert Schumann appealed to this symphony in his own proposal of marriage to Clara Wieck. And he wrote:

> Everyone must recognise, while listening to this symphony, that it reveals to us something more than mere beauty, mere joy and sorrow. Here we find, beside the most masterly technicalities of musical composition, life in every vein; colouring down to the finest gradation; meaning everywhere, sharp expression in every detail. . . .
>
> And then the heavenly length of the symphony, like that of a thick novel in four volumes, perhaps by Jean Paul who also was never able to reach a conclusion, and for the best reason – to permit the reader to think it out for himself. How this refreshes, this feeling of abundance . . . the entirely new world that opens before us.

Now, Schumann doesn't quite hit the nub of the matter. Schubert's writing was never more richly variegated than here;

but its bounding rhythmic spring gives a majestic cohesion, something easy and gracefully splendid, to the widest range of interludes. Once its proportions and its symmetry have been understood, it is a piece whose thinking is impeccably concise. Its appetite for life and sense of pace, the sweep with which it carries off its own weight, mean that it is not a minute too long.

The disembodied call with which two horns open the symphony has a familiar ring. It borrows the rhythm used by Schubert to set Goethe's '*Gesang der Geister über den Waßern*' and also '*Die Allmacht*' – Schubert's song of praise to the Creator, which was written in August 1825. As John Reed observed:

> *The primordial hymn which announces the theme of the* 'Great' C major *is a hymn to the glory of to the natural world. . . . Its pages bear the imprint everywhere of his romantic feeling for natural beauty, both in its total conception and in detail. Nobody who has heard the notes of the traditional alpenhorn echoing round the mountain valleys can doubt where Schubert found the inspiration for 'the horns of Elfland faintly blowing' which so magically illumine the first movement.*

In all its moods – serene, bucolic, or in the exhilarated *perpetuum mobile* of its finale – this is a symphony brought to life by song; but a song of grander breadth, sonorous power and sustained fervour than could be heard before or since.

It used to be thought that the *Grand Duo in C*, D812 (June 1824) was a transcription for duet of a Gmunden-Gastein symphony that had been lost. Such is the richness of Schubert's piano music in these years. He tried his hand at four piano sonatas: melodic as ever in their impulses, ever more unified in their themes, more cogent in their manipulation of themes. The first of them, in C major (D840: April 1825), is unfinished – hence its nickname of '*Reliquié*'.

This is the first sonata to show the extraordinary spaciousness of Schubert's later instrumental music. Confidence, a sense of striding out into nature, is as marked as in the '*Wanderer*' *Fantasy*, but with lyricism in place of the earlier fevered display. There is a hint of *Alice through the Looking Glass* as the listener is led through a series of remote keys, to a last-minute twist. The second movement is even more surprising: a cradle-song that is interrupted by explosive interludes, with quirky harmonic delights en route. After that, there are only sketches.

The overall plan and opening theme of the *A minor Sonata*, D845, come from the same stock; but its emotional affinities lie with the A minor work of two years before. It is as if D784 were the frozen glacial egg from which a work of art has germinated: if by art we mean, as Henry James did, 'a mind in dialogue with itself' or as Schoenberg believed, the expression of significant emotional experience through an organism with an anatomy, a life of its own, a function and reason for being. In D845 the most intimate and the most massive perspectives are aligned through an act of unfolding consciousness in which optimism always fails. It is an event as private and as public as our own mortality. A trio as naive as a fable is pitted against a structure of brutal force: the private meditation of the slow movement's variations – only one instance of the sonata's stupendous capacity for transmutation – offers a fleeting glimpse of wounded innocence, the memory of some faraway thing that is more intense for having been violated.

If D845 has the closeness of a confession, the next sonata (D major, D850: August 1825) is Schubert at his most ceremonial. It was written as a display-piece for a virtuoso pianist, Karl Maria von Bocklet. Thematic emptiness is not a charge you can often lay against Schubert, but perhaps that is the case in the opening here. Nor is it the issue, because he uses the clash of major and minor to generate one of his most impressive structures. The benevolent slow movement shoots red blood into the Larghetto of Beethoven's *Second Symphony*, but it is in the Scherzo that one becomes aware of an agenda hidden beneath the surface. Its opening bars are mock-heroic, and the final Allegro moderato trots away with angelic sweetness. No wonder Schumann was appalled by this little game. For Schumann, thinking like a child came naturally. For Schubert, it is a matter of guile.

The *molto moderato e cantabile* of the *Sonata in G major*, D894 (October 1826) has the same mysterious poise as '*Du bist die Ruh*' ' and '*Im Abendrot*', an ethereal calmness that suggests time standing still, as it does in the opening of Beethoven's *Fourth Piano Concerto*. Both this and the slow movement use dramatic interventions to galvanize placid opening themes, which then resolve in warm affection. It is contemporary with the quartet in the same key, yet it has the relationship to Schubert's piano music that

Beethoven's Opus 95 has to his chamber music: a transitional essay, which looks forward to Schubert's last months while being a delight in itself.

The Rondo finale has the quality of bells across a meadow. This time Schumann was at his most perceptive. 'If anyone has not the imagination to solve the riddle of the last movement, let him leave it alone.' And of the sonata as a whole? 'In form and spirit, it is the most perfect work.'

SCHUBERT AND SONG

Are Schubert's songs for chorus no more than neglected manuscripts for a dead form of music-making? If so, the loss is ours. '*Die Nacht*' (D983: 'See how the clear stars move in the meadows of heaven') evokes phosphorescent stillness within its first bar. '*Wehmuth*' ('Melancholy', D825) is about the atmosphere that envelopes a mood. Then the nuances of words can look after themselves; for a developing tonality means that upon scene-painting Schubert is able to fuse a story of one individual's loss with consistent fatalism. He summons the Romantic conception of life and death within a pastoral landscape, unified by the rhythm of a tolling bell, and no other composer could make a major key sound quite so pitiable. The dissolving musical contexts of '*Nachthelle*' (D892) allow Schubert to depict first the earth, then the spellbound poet, and a lambent field of constellations. Within fifteen minutes, all three pieces are over. Yet each is a macrocosm: and if Mahler claimed that a symphony should be like the world, we have been made aware that for Schubert every song is a world.

As Richard Capell used to say: Schubert had eyes, he glanced rapidly, and he took in the main features of a poet's scene as no musician before him had done. A hint of landscape, of atmosphere, or of an accompanying movement or gesture, 'struck his fancy and started in him picturesque figures of a unique vividness.' His song-writing represents a special agreement between music and verse unlike any known before or since.

Above everything his songs are meditations, not meant to address a crowd, but discovering delight in new poetry and a new instrument. He was exhilarated by it, engrossed: and like Beethoven he conceived the developing piano as an orchestra. Comparisons of the keyboard writing of either to passages for strings, brass or drums, are not fanciful. Yet the piano is an oblique instrument, a chimerical instrument. Its voice lacks colour. It veers between sensuous communication and an idea of music, an abstraction: and precisely because of that – not in spite of it – the piano calls up a suggestive potency beyond its resources.

False to assume, then, that the pianist in a Schubert song is an accompanist. Singer and instrumentalist are on different planes, joined in an act of communion between equals, in a symbiosis that neither alone can more than hint at. In many of Schubert's songs the melodic line is not self-supporting, but glows through the figures and harmonies with which it is associated, their rhythmic agitations and developing emotional suggestion. It would be as facile to dismiss him as a melodist as it is to label him a classicist.

Schubert's songs are related to the *Lieder* of the past only by the anaemic formalities they negate: by their discovery of simple, indivisible, invincible dramatic movement. In '*Im Abendrot*' or '*Litanei*' the sheer quality of the long vocal line, shorn of virtuosity and all extraneous effect, is never in doubt. In '*Der Atlas*' (D957) he hugs every word, but things are not as simple as that. The kernel of the song is a line well into Heine's poem, '*Eine Welt, die ganze Welt*' ('A world, the whole miserable world, is my burden') and for this key phrase Schubert has devised a welling motive, a gathering of force which his introduction must anticipate like a prophecy, and from which the remainder of the song must grow. So it does. Schubert matches metre and poetic import to achieve an embodiment of Romanticism's *Zeitgeist*, its defining worldview.

In his *Lieder*, Schubert aligns music and Romantic literature, to represent what has been called subjectivity in action. By this I mean more than an act of eager artistic engagement. The aim of a Romantic song is not to enhance the emotional force of the text, nor even to refashion its meaning by either direct or ironic means. The purpose is, as Lawrence Kramer has put it, 'to represent the activity of a unique subject: conscious, self-conscious, and unconscious, whose experience takes place as a series of conflicts and reconciliations between inner and outer reality.' The subject of Romantic poetry, according to Wordsworth, is a 'mighty mind' which 'feeds upon infinity', bent on a mission no less than to enlarge the historical and the personal concept of self, to articulate the voice of the self. To quote *The Prelude* (1805), such a mind is:

> *Ever on the watch*
> *Willing to work and to be wrought upon....*
> *Exalted by an underpresence*
> *The sense of God, or whosoe'er is dim*
> *And vast in its own being.*

A voice for the self, then. But whose voice? The persona of the composer himself, speaking through the music, but standing apart from it? No, not necessarily; nor the persona of the poet, the text. Above either of them stands something summoned for the occasion, a music with a life of its own that affirms itself by recasting the rhetoric, rhythm and imagery of the text on its own terms: investing it with the 'magical power' of imagination described by Samuel Taylor Coleridge, which 'dissolves, diffuses, dissipates, in order to re-create'. The movement of a song corresponds to this process of fresh creation, where the composer's imagination encounters another thinking entity, which it may accept or repudiate. It is an encounter between the self and a kaleidoscope of other opportunities, other personified self-images, other possibilities in knowing.

Classical tonality is in the business of resolution: making clear, making good, making simple. Not so for Schubert. His songs recurrently incorporate a conflict between Classical tonality and harmonic innovation, which never quite escapes its Classical origins, yet draws them beyond a system, beyond a dialogue between systems. His songs are a human testament – Classicism parodied, saluted, betrayed and made uncanny. They are an arena for clashing perspectives, where what seemed natural is exposed, stripped to the bones, appropriated, or left alone. Where he leaves things well alone, his ingenuousness is not simple, but sophisticated. '*Heidenröslein*', charming though it might be, is not the invention of an innocent. Quite as much as the D850 *Piano Sonata*, the *Lieder* are a feat of metacommunication; by which I mean, a commentary on the presumptions upon which a body of experience depends and with them, the means by which it can be expanded, recrafted, brought down.

We see this most dramatically in those through-composed

songs where Schubert splits the composition into disjunctive halves which, at the end, are tenuously reconciled by a few perfunctory measures of what Kramer calls 'tonal circling', through a cycle of keys that floats desultorily in the direction of home. So '*Einsamkeit*' (from *Winterreise*), begins with bleak detachment, framed in a mordant impaction of harmonies. Its second section is a jagged display of shifting dynamics. Twice the music struggles towards a climax, and the credulous tonality of the opening gains a bitter and frustrated agitation. Its frame of reference has changed: truth has broken through just as at seems we were about to fall into a fool's oblivion. This is a song about learning a lesson, about being the same but changed. What games of subtle mystification Schubert plays, and what clarity of perception they bring.

Classicism is, for Schubert, the flickering background before which he plays out his lonely dramas. Edmund Husserl, a phenomenologist, introduced the concept of 'horizon', by which he meant the tacitly apprehended context of lived experience. In '*Die Stadt*' (D957), where the poet glimpses a town from his boat, classical structures represent the security of the past, and harmony threatens to collapse with the poet's sanity: when the sun rises, the light of day reveals only the profundity of lost love, a neurotic re-enactment of failure. But there are none of the histrionics by which Tchaikovsky or Mahler would announce their latest bout of ostentatious self-pity. Schubert's harmonic vacillation places him in a different league of genius; and with him we end as we began, in an impressionistic haze of existential dread.

Why are there so many songs about nature? Partly because the evaporating tone of the early piano lends itself to rapid and watery figurations, whose changing currents suit a mind of Schubert's darting inventiveness. But no, not really. Schubert is an artist who deals in shared experience, but the experience of his fellow men as an extension of nature: nature as the gateway to the world of the spirit which, for the Romantics, was a higher reality, yet nature too as a force implacable in its capacity for cruelty and dissolution. Just as Schubert was a social animal enlightened and destroyed by the activities of his friends (and there is so much of their poetry in his hymns to creation), so it was to predestination that he owed everything, including his knowledge of his own appalling fate. Primeval diversity and renewal might serve as an emblem for human hope, its energy for the fact that each of us is ultimately and horribly alone; but for Schubert there was a more immediate significance. It was the force with which his vital urges ebbed and flowed.

Take a letter written from Vienna in 1826:

> *I am not working at all – the weather here is truly appalling. The Almighty seems to have forsaken us altogether, for the sun refuses to shine. It is May, and we cannot sit in any garden yet. Appalling! Ghastly! And the most cruel thing on earth for me.*

What more could we expect from a syphilitic, whose body was corroding as his vision became more acute, whose decay fluctuated with the cycle of seasons?

Seen in this light, a symbol of fidelity and modesty (and this is what Dame's Violets, the flower of Aphrodite, meant to Schubert) serves too as a token of clinging through thick and thin. An image of poisoned love, as well; but that came after the composing of '*Nachtviolen*' (D752) in 1823. Yet on any evidence, '*Nachtviolen*' is no longer a song about a flower. It addresses a significant element in our moral predicament. It is about a land of childlike rapture, of purity and the vulnerability of innocence. And this, distilled into music, lies at the heart of its sense of balm within haunted and suspended time.

The rococo elegance of '*Gott im Frühlinge*' (D448), fresh with the nascent energy of rising sap, is more than a pantheist's nostalgia for an age in which emotion was apprehended more simply and clearly than it is for us. It finds Schubert's most optimistic recognition of what could never be regained. 'Art concealing art', it has been said of this song: and so, inimitably, it is. No wonder the Viennese used to complain that 'this time the popular composer has gone too far.' The universe of his thinking – the universality of his themes – was as far beyond their perception as the stars through which Schulze, in his poem '*Der Liebliche Stern*' (D861) explores a decline into madness. Schubert's significance is in the fact that his music is never contained in its form; its modernity is in its zeal and its intangibility, the fact that nothing can be taken for granted.

The persona of the Harper's Songs, an outcast beneath the wandering moon, is not an isolated artistic event. The withered leaves and pathetic fallacy of '*Die Blumen Schmerz*' ('The flowers' pain', D731) and '*Die Blumensprache*' ('The language of flowers', D519), their sense of violation ('flowers proclaim our suffering') portend a desire for death. The rose ('*Die Rose*', D745) is a symbol of purity to mark the progress of a living being on the path to eternal cold. In '*Nach einem Gewitter*' (D561) the felicities of natural order (embodied in harmony) shine like a string of pearls: the stars are tokens of constancy beyond a world of self-delusion, part of an infinity with which we can commune. In '*Die Sterne*' (D176) Johann Fellinger asks, 'You stars, so noble and so fair; What drives you on your dark course through the blue ocean of the ether?' And in '*Am See*' Bruchmann speculates,

> *If man becomes a lake,*
> *Stars, oh so many stars*
> *Will fall from the gates of heaven*
> *Into the play of waves within his soul.*

With the pristine insight of an outsider Schubert's music is lifted into a timelessness that the faded sentiments of its literary sources could never attain. Listen to '*Der Liebliche Stern*' and you realize that he has no need to follow every nuance of these words. This is because each song presents a world-view that is pervasive and compelling. Schubert gives us a portrait, not of a mood, but of what it is like to be such a person. The richness of his suggestion – the tingle of empathy between Schubert's experience and our own – makes for artistry of a supreme calibre. But what makes it magical is its sense of contradictions assimilated and made fertile. The words of '*Auf dem Waßer zu singen*' (D774) might almost be his epitaph: 'May time disappear on shimmering wings: I vanish myself from changing time.' The half-light of ambivalence, the sense of stasis within motion, of languor within palpitating ardour: all of this, polished between Classical discipline and Romantic contemplation, adds to Schubert's unique lucidity and stature.

The moment of dusk is a special one for Schubert. To a Romantic thinker the world apprehended through our senses was simply a hieroglyph for one beyond. The function of the artist was to lead us to the frontier between the seen and the unseen, to express that longing for the world of the spirit which the

Romantics called *Sehnsucht*. Nature stands at this barrier as the omnipotence of truth, and its discovery as truth to oneself. As Stolberg says in '*Auf dem Waßer zu singen* ':

> *The soul, too, glides like a boat*
> *For from the sky the setting sun*
> *Dances upon the waves around the boat. . . .*
> *The soul breathes the joys of heaven,*
> *The peace of the grove, in the reddening glow.*

In the night Schubert finds release from the magniloquent dogmas of his age, and takes flight in diaphanous suggestibility. There, more than anywhere else, he takes the hedonism of the Viennese and makes it into a sort of sublimity. Nightfall, to Schubert, is not a time of misgivings or the oppression of thickened light. It is a time of dancing brightness, for fantasy and moral reappraisal, freedom to overturn the incontrovertible truths of the day. It brings out the best in him, as it did in Yeats and Samuel Palmer: nocturnes, fables, an occasion for whispered and discovered intimacies beneath rustling leaves and the songs of nightingales: a chance for introspection touched with benevolent mystery. In '*An den Mond*' (D259) the moon nourishes the night to give solace to the happy man 'who, without hatred, shuts himself off from the world.' In '*Stimme der Liebe*' (D418), a moment of flaming expectancy seems to materialize in the summer night:

> *Come, fair Laura!*
> *Flowers bloom at her airy footsteps*
> *And like the music of the spheres*
> *The sweet voice of love*
> *Floats tremulously towards me from the roses of her lips.*

Brahms said, 'There is not one of Schubert's songs from which you cannot learn something.' But another musician put it less prosaically. 'It takes a rather good composer,' he wrote, 'to catch the sound of starlight.'

CHAPTER 8
SWANSONG
(1827–28)

+ Winterreise; Schwanengesang
+ Late, short pieces
+ Three great piano sonatas; the C major Quintet
+ Schubert's death

February 1827 saw Schubert dejected, worn out. As the year passed he was to show increasing symptoms of the old malaise, but for now, something else was tapping his energies. Spaun takes up the story:

> Schubert had been in a sombre mood for some time. When I asked him what was wrong, he would only say, 'Now, you will all soon hear and understand.' One day he said to me, 'Come to Schober's today. I shall sing you a cycle of frightful songs. I'm curious to see what you will all say about them. They have taken more out of me than was ever the case before.' He then sang us the whole Winterreise with great emotion.
>
> We were taken aback by their dark mood, and Schober declared that he had liked only one of them, Der Lindenbaum. To that Schubert only said: 'I like these songs better than all the others and one day you will fall for them too.' And he was right; we were won over by the impression made by these profound songs which Vogl sang in a masterly way.

History has tended to agree with Schober. 'The Lime Tree' soon gained the status of a popular ballad, its invitation to suicide discreetly underplayed; but only in the twentieth century has the cycle been recognized as the greatest inspiration of the greatest song-writer, and performed complete. For above all these are poems for winter, composed in the shadow of winter. One could call *Winterreise* a musical novella about time, and be right so to do. But it is also the work of a man whose sickness and vicissitudes have left him utterly alone, who can save himself only by making his own moribund desires into something better.

Both *Winterreise* and '*Die schöne Müllerin*' are about broken love, and both correspond to critical stages in Schubert's syphilis. The winter's journey starts at a later point in the story: the course of a young man's love is already behind him, and the work opens on his leaving the town where his love still lives, without his even seeing her again. *Winterreise* is much more sparse in texture than '*Die schöne Müllerin*'. It is has fewer of those strophic songs which spread their wings expansively and come to a comforting close. *Winterreise* traces a bleak trajectory towards death.

The Winter's Journey is the story of a realist who confronts his lack of self-knowledge until the puzzle of his destiny is vouchsafed to him. This is in the final song, where he approaches a hurdy-gurdy man shivering in bare feet on the icy outskirts of a town from which he has been driven by dogs. Before that encounter the wanderer has not met a soul. He speaks to the river, a crow, the snarling dogs, the snow. But they never reply as they would in *Märchen* – the sentimental and supernatural tales of Schubert's day. The objectivity is unremitting, as it must be for us to eavesdrop on the monologues of a private extinction. The wanderer's name is never revealed, the events of his life are already past. He is an outline stumbling in a snowstorm.

Time is rarely measurable. We gather that between '*Im Dorfe*' and '*Der stürmische Morgen*' a night has passed. We never know what distance the wanderer has travelled. The journey unfolds within a cocoon of private and fractured sentience whose introspection, whose corrosive interrogation of every emotion, is rooted in the wanderer's sense of estrangement from the world and from himself. It is a glimmer of emotional, not logical, episodes. Each song depicts a stage in the lover's experience, where a specific state of mind is reflected by the austerity of the winter landscape. Many of the songs have little if any physical movement, although the poet observes other things: a carrion bird circling overhead, the last leaf dropping. The focus is drawn inwards to concentrate on a psychic journey, the journey of life itself whose twists and turns, whose pain and final loss, are reflected and illuminated in images of Nature. The fleeting memory of hope is a glint of iridescent water: the endless present of the final songs, with the numbed horror of eyes that cannot close and which are condemned to live and to witness, is echoed in the grinding of a machine that 'no one wants to hear'.

It is the panorama of organic life, organic forces, that gives this human plight its universality. To Schubert, as to all Romantics, the ardour of love (its heightened sensory awareness) allows empathy with a natural world in which feelings find their correspondence. With *Winterreise* a direct parallel is drawn between external and internal nature – which Schubert underlines musically by means of texture and dissonance, by continuities and breaks in the vocal line. Schubert's sense of context was never more eloquent than it is here. He reverses Wilhelm Müller's order for '*Mut*' ('Courage') and '*Die Nebensonnen*' ('The phantom suns') so as to follow false cheer and bravado with a cryptic lament for the light that has drained from the poet's life. This sets the stage for the meeting with a starving musician.

The country walk, and its ideology of a direct contact with Nature through physical activity pushed to the point of exhaustion, dominated German literature from the mid-eighteenth century to the Second World War. No surprise, then, that images of walking dominate the first half of the cycle here, many of whose songs suggest its rhythm. Over this movement, Schubert imposes the musical images of landscape – for '*Mein Herz*' a frozen stream, beneath which feeling still flows. It is the symbol of the poet's heart. Beyond exhaustion, in the second half, is the intimation of death: so that the piano figuration for the raven, which hovers above the voice, descends finally into earth.

Winterreise is unsurpassed in the art of musical representation. A signpost (or '*Wegweiser*') is the formal announcement of death, and it induces in its rigidity of line a sense of imminent terror. As Charles Rosen put it:

> *Throughout* Winterreise, *the dynamic processes of nature are represented by musical landscape painting of extraordinary suggestion and even precision: the pivoting of the weathervane, the flowing water under ice, the rustling of leaves, the winter wind, the will-o'-the-wisp, the slowly moving clouds, the quiet*

village street, a stormy morning – all these receive a remarkable musical contour. As in the great landscape tradition, present sensation and memory are superimposed and confounded. Above all, it is the sense of future time that Müller and Schubert have added to the physical sense of the present and the past.

Now, Schubert flourished in the climate established by Goethe's novel *The Sorrows of Young Werther*, a warning against the devastating consequences of unbridled sensibility in which a young artist was brought down by unconsummated love. In turn, *Winterreise* is the forerunner of Schoenberg's expressionist *Erwantung* and its retreat from pain into the labyrinths of the self. Yet *Winterreise* is unique. It begins with the door slammed implacably in its face; no other music has quite its capacity to invest the major with the colour, the afterglow, of desolation and disillusionment.

Schubert understood the verbal extravagance of Müller's verses and knew he had to pare his own language back to its simplest. The appearance of E major for '*Der Lindenbaum*' brings home with painful immediacy, after the minor keys of opening songs, the happiness of the past. The melodic line of '*Der greise Kopf*' draws a silhouette in music. The ending brings an unemotional pause on the brink of insanity. In these final moments Schubert seems to reveal his familiarity with the maimed and staring numbness of terminal depression, its weariness and the corrupted wariness that come with recognizing the heart of darkness within a life's landmarks, standing silent and consumed as if with the enormity of an unremembered crime.

The world, then, is a thing observed and reflected on as an extension of the wanderer's emotional state, rather than as something that can be either objectively perceived or actively engaged. This ambiguity, a characteristic of Romantic poetry and prose, becomes an abundance for Schubert in which the rational is interpenetrated by the poetic, the present with the past; and reality by emotion, imagination, recollection. Barbara Barry has shown that the use of major keys can be understood in terms of these loops back into memory, which bring solace by replacing temporarily the present reality of alienation and winter. Major keys towards the end of *Winterreise* are used to demonstrate how the distinction between past and present, between external and internal reality, have dissolved. The wanderer sees the landscape before him entirely through the perspective of his own melancholic perceptions.

Barry argues that *Winterreise* does not take place on any single level, but on many levels of time and experience. There's physical time, of course, marked by actions and by events. There is remembered time: the gates of memory opened – in a Proustian way – by the sight of some particular object. There is experiential time too, an ebb and flow of feeling. In the end, there is inertia only.

These levels of time correspond to various levels of the journey. There is the physical journey, but the psychic journey too: with its emotional swings and arbitrary associations. Then there are what Barry calls lacunae, deviations into memory which have the burning intensity of hallucinations. In the end, again, there is only dissolution: where death is awaited, but where it has not yet arrived.

The dream-time of *Winterreise* is essential to its structure. Barbara Barry suggests that the second half takes the experiences of the first and transforms them through memory. '*Im Dorfe*' ('In the village') revisits the place abandoned in '*Gute Nacht*'. The angry bite of '*Mut*' takes the place of Frühlingstraum's naive reminiscence. '*Letzte Hoffnung*' ('A last hope') expresses the lowest ebb of grief, but at least it has the fight left in it for that: its counterpart, '*Der Leiermann*' seems to inhabit the Ninth Circle of Danté's hell, whose inmates lie forever in ice.

Yet the fate of the wanderer is not sealed. His final question is to the organ-grinder: 'Strange old man, shall I go with you? Will you grind your organ to my singing?' It is Schubert's destiny, too, to be a musician – his means of survival in a hostile world. In the writing of E.T.A. Hoffmann, fellow musicians recognize each other instinctively, without any need of words. Secret bonds ('*geheimes Beziehungen*') unite them in shared experience. For Müller too, the musician is the highest common factor of universalized human experience: master of his future, choosing his own lonely road, yet able to reach out from the depths and touch humankind.

THE LAST SHORT PIECES

Winterreise sets out the geography of Schubert's world. It brings what was always there to new heights of expression, and has profound implications for everything that must follow.

Always there? From the time of '*Erlkönig*' Schubert had juxtaposed two perspectives: the illusion of bright and beautiful dreams, the reality of what was wretched, threatening, banal. In Erlkönig a supernatural being utters soft blandishments to a storm-tossed child, and the demon alone is given seductive music. The creak of Gretchen's spinning wheel is a materialization of what is real to her. Rückert's '*Daß sie hier gewesen*' (1823), concerned as so often with tragic reminiscence, prevaricates between keys until the memory of the loved one allows it to break through into the major. This modulation – a spiritual as well as tonal contrast – is what gives Schubert's songs their psychological depth.

But *Winterreise* is something new: the product of an artistic second childhood, where superlative effect and simplicity co-exist. What *Winterreise* is about is the sorrow latent in human illusions. The suggestion of physical movement in '*Wegweiser*' ('The signpost') is grim reality, the processional trudge to death: pure melody ('*Täuschung*', or 'Illusion') is our capacity to experience joy in spite of the pain of loss.

How much this duality means to Schubert in his last months! It recurs in the stoicism of the D929 *Piano Trio*'s slow movement: and in the anaesthetized grief of Heine's '*Ihr Bild*' ('Her picture', one of the songs gathered after Schubert's death into *Schwanengesang*, D957), where imagination is all we have to console us against the desolation brought about by time. This for Schubert is what being alive means: that residue of consciousness that registers the inconstancy of experience against its own, constant being; and its implications take us far beyond his songs.

The F minor *Fantasy for four hands* (D940: March 1828) is dedicated to Caroline Esterházy, the retarded aristocrat whom Schubert adored, and who was trundling her hoop round the streets of Vienna long after his death. Its opening theme suggests the rhythm and intonation of speech, a forlorn conversation. The overall quality of the music is narrative, it evokes the landscape of ceaseless wandering familiar from the two Müller cycles. Illusion is shattered by a plunge into the minor key, as in '*Erlkönig*', and redeemed briefly by memory. Just as much as *Winterreise*, the *Fantasy* is haunted by a progress towards an inescapable destiny. Schubert appropriates poetic content from his songs and transforms it into a purely musical structure for what is surely the greatest of all piano duets.

David Lewin revealed the techniques by which the same composer, in '*Auf dem Fluße*' (D911 No.7), could evoke a false exterior of motion and warmth, with a frozen heart within. Yet that is Schubert's artistic guise, which he adopts quite as calculatedly as Wordsworth or Browning. At the same time, he was planning two of his happiest pieces [i.e. the *Piano Trios*]. The last song he wrote, '*Die Taubenpost*' ('The pigeon post', D957 No.14) and '*Im Frühling*' (D882), which lacerates the heart, are confirmation enough.

Schumann wrote in excitement of the discovery of the *B flat Piano Trio* (D898, 1828): 'One glance at Schubert's *Trio* – and the troubles of our human existence disappear and all the world is fresh and bright again. Yet ten years ago a trio by Schubert passed across the face of the musical world like some angry meteor. . . . To sum up: the *Trio in E flat* is active, masculine, dramatic, while the *B flat* is passive, feminine, lyrical.

If in the *B flat Trio* Schumann was trying to highlight both a voluptuous and ardent vulnerability at work, how right he was. It is as strange as most of Schubert's music must have seemed, in a world still filled with Mozart and Beethoven. This trio is one of Vienna's most quicksilver apparitions, where a gossamer lightness of texture often seems charged with brilliant sonority. The gloss of eagerness and yearning: the impulsive gallops up and down the keyboard and exuberant asides: the martial rhythms and childlike confidences (often dissolving into each other) give it a quality beyond joy. What I mean is that the piece has a sort of knowing innocence, and this creates a conversation between equals of special intimacy.

The happy fusion of opposites, then, makes it deftly elusive; and this is what we, as much as Schubert's contemporaries, boil down to the myth of 'sociability'. Its first movement is a paraphrase of a song from 1825, '*Des Sängers Habe*': 'Shatter my joy in pieces, take from me all my worldly goods, yet leave me only my zither and I shall be happy and rich.' Its final Rondo derives from the 1815 '*Skolie*' (D306): 'Let us, in the bright May morning, take delight in the life of the flower, before its fragrance disappears.'

The *E flat Trio* (D929, November 1827) is certainly more extrovert, but the theme from the Andante slow movement, when it reappears in the finale, is one of Schubert's most gorgeous exercises in euphony. His wish to foster a sense of unity from the first bar to the last is clear, and its structure is one of the most adventurous he drafted. Difficult, perhaps, not to be reminded of the symphonies: the *Ninth*'s boisterous abundance, tempered with the melodic poignancy of the '*Unfinished*'. Perhaps the wanderer steps out a little more circumspectly this time.

But the music the public remembers most affectionately from the final twelve months are two sets of four *Impromptus* (D899, D935, both late 1827). They are lovely outpourings of song-without-words, in which mercurial asides, the sense of a hairpin bend of changing nuance and brighter possibilities, find their place in narratives of seamless inevitability. They are music whose humanity is all the more moving for being heard through Schubert's customary twilight glow of ambivalence: emotion cooled or reflected from another surface, as Schubert's music so often is.

It is tempting to think of them as artless, but wrong. In their lustrous sound they show Schubert's gift in writing for the developing Viennese pianos of his day, and they are extended essays that grow out of initial impulses, generally rhythmic gestures presented in the opening bars. The first four quietly dazzle in their daring key-relationships: the second set exists on a bigger scale, and is more varied in structure. The opening Impromptu of D935, in F minor, is an incarnation of flowing water, like '*Liebesbotschaft*' ('Love's message' – D957 No.1); the second is a moment of contemplation that takes flight. The third, in B flat, is a series of sparkling variations.

Schwanengesang ('Swansong'), is the sentimental title given to Schubert's last settings of Rellstab, Heine and Seidl when they were collected after his death. They are as fine as anything he wrote, but something is new: the conversational role of the accompanying piano, which engenders new intimacy and a new depth. '*Frühlingssehnsucht*' ('Longing for the Spring', No.3) and '*Kriegers Ahnung*' (No.2) could come respectively from '*Die schöne Müllerin*' and Schubert's Ossian settings of many years before, but for these extra layers of meaning, which might be peeled back like the skin of an onion. The order of the Heine settings is Schubert's own, and beyond its cumulative charge there is also the chemistry by which each song affects its neighbours, as if we are digging deeper into the strata of a secret tragedy.

In '*Der Atlas*' (No.8) the poet wipes his former love from his mind, only to see her portrait ('*Ihr Bild* '), in a projection of fantasy upon reality, comes to life and writes its imprint in tears. In '*Die Stadt* ' (No.11) he sees her town from the water: '*Am Meer*' ('By the sea', No.12) presents past consummation as a metaphor for spiritual and physical decay; in '*Der Doppelgänger* ' (No.13) the poet stands before her house and sees only his own spectre. The open harmonies of '*Das Fischermädchen* ' give optimism the raw brightness of a myth: the tonal compactness of '*Am Meer*' marks the consoling sobriety of inward realization, and the passage of time, after the catatonic grief of '*Die Stadt* ' with its ghostly rhythm of oars through sombre light. '*Am Meer* ' catches the poet at the moment of redefinition, between the fading and careless hopes of '*Das Fischermädchen* ' and a poisoned kiss. After this, the only outcome can be the terror of self-recognition.

The composer who could write such things was on the verge of a breakthrough of major stature within the history of music. It paves the way, in his last *Piano Sonatas* and the *String Quintet*, to music not of discovery, but of self-discovery.

By the end of 1827, Schubert was slipping into the background of Viennese life, and letters addressed to simply 'Franz Schubert, composer' were likely to be delivered to his namesake, a local violinist. But there was one moment of triumph, when on 26 March 1828 a large and enthusiastic audience applauded a concert of his songs and the new *E Flat Trio*. Encouraged, Schubert began to plan his final instrumental masterpieces.

THE LAST GREAT WORKS

Beethoven died in March 1827. Schubert, always too shy to introduce himself during his idol's lifetime, was one of the pallbearers at the funeral.

According to Johann Leopold Ebner, Schubert was once on the point of excising one of his own songs because a friend had drawn his attention to a few measures that unconsciously quoted Beethoven's '*Coriolan*' Overture. The year was 1817, the music was '*Die Forelle*', which the young composer had just finished. 'Schubert saw this at once, too, and wanted to destroy the song, but we would not allow it and thus we saved that glorious piece from destruction.'

A sign of artistic insecurity? If so, why had Schubert been so happy to base the opening movement of his *Second Symphony* on

Beethoven's *First*? The creative relationship between the two composers is full of paradoxes. Beethoven was from the outset the measure of all things to Schubert: a role-model, a daunting creative block, a spur, and in the end, the yardstick against which he could assess his own stature and identity. For the truth is that, with the older man's death, Schubert embarked upon a rivalry from which he had shrunk in the lifetime of the one whom he held in awe and reverence.

The last trilogy of Schubert's *Piano Sonatas* (D.958–60) was written in the space of one month, September 1828. Perhaps Schubert was drawn towards making some tribute? The first *Sonata* of the three, in *C minor*, begins with a quotation from Beethoven's thirty-two *Variations in C minor*, and its presence underlines Schubert's assumption of a Beethovenian posture. The finale of Schubert's last *sonata* of all, in *B flat*, has many points in common with Beethoven's quartet in the same key (Op.130), beyond a shared and dance-like metre.

But the most intriguing parallel is yet to come. Between them Edward Cone and Charles Rosen have demonstrated that the Rondo of the *A major Sonata*, D959, is a homage to that of Beethoven's *Piano Sonata No.1*, Op.31, modelled so precisely that the act of plagiarism can only be deliberate. The opening theme has the same contour: the pianistic figuration is the same, so is the counterpoint, the rhythm, and so is the formal structure.

Why? Is the answer that Schubert's finales caused him problems (many of his unfinished sonatas came to grief in them) and that he sought an easy exemplar? Such a casual act of appropriation – dishonesty, even – does not square easily with the protest, from Schubert's deathbed, that he was being neglected because he did not lie near Beethoven. Neither does it account for the the systematic changes which Schubert works on his model. Schubert's unforced melodic expansiveness stretches his second theme out of all proportion; as Cone puts it, 'he dwells lovingly' on each bare element that Beethoven has offered him, creating moments of remembrance and magic. The stage is the same: the voice rebounds in a different world.

What is remarkable, declares Rosen, is the imitation's lack of inhibitions: the ease and confidence with which Schubert moves within his pre-ordained cage. His structural borrowings exist on a purely formal level, as indeed a sonnet does; they are moulds into which he can pour his own inspirations. Mahler spoke of Schubert's 'freedom below the surface of convention'. There is nothing slavish in Schubert, nothing docile: his innovations are not extensions of classical style but, as Rosen has shown, completely new inventions. Crowning everything is his discovery of the oscillation between two tonal levels to achieve a stasis in which time itself is redefined. We need to return and explore this properly; but for now it is enough to say that Beethoven's aims, and Schubert's, are fundamentally different.

Sketches for these last sonatas show how scrupulously, how self-critically, Schubert proceeded. His 'heavenly lengths' appear obsessive only when he means them to be. But classical forms define boundaries, and the space that Schubert needs in order to move freely has little to do with classical definitions. In the first movement of the D958 *Sonata in C minor* he lingers on harmonic riches and then goads them into developments on a symphonic scale: apparent asides are seized and made part of a process of melodic evolution which anticipates Berlioz, Liszt, Tchaikovsky: in the finale, modulations pile on each other with an insistence that had never been conceived of before. If there is any of Beethoven left in this, it is Beethoven reduced to a pathology, and steeped in the frightful hallucinations of Goya.

As Alfred Brendel argues, 'Schubert relates to Beethoven, he reacts to him, but he follows him hardly at all. Models are concealed, transformed, surpassed.' For Schubert, classicism means music for music's sake: empowered by its own tensions, its discipline and resources, existing for itself. In that sense, he becomes a more classical composer – not less – as he matures. But this is classicism of what might be called a quietly apocalyptic kind. Brendel continues, 'Order, even when only an adornment through which the chaos of emotion shines, is decisive because it makes the work of art possible.' For Schubert classical form is a shadowy life-in-death, a decorum and a ritual which – like the signpost in *Winterreise* – marks the direction of a solitary agenda.

Rosen suggests that, with the finale of the *A major Sonata*, Schubert produces a work 'that is unquestionably greater than its model.' I think we may be a little unfair to Beethoven, who mischievously and wittily diverted the formalities of what his audience took for granted in order to create what has been called the first neo-classical sonata. Yet it is also time for us to celebrate

Schubert's essential indeterminacy not as an intimation of weakness, but (as much as in *Schwanengesang*) the language of music's first truly modern artist.

The last piano sonatas stand as a family, marked off by their poetry and grandeur of conception: the first of them terse, the second a ballade-like web of sound and movement in some ethereal form, the last of the three serenely contemplative and tinged with grave romantic yearning. Their progression of keys too corresponds to a kind of perfect cadence, a psychological progress into resignation and light. More puzzling than the imprint of Beethoven is the profusion of self-quotations and allusions. In the *A major* work the theme of the finale is lifted from the Allegretto of the *A minor Sonata* (D537) of 1817, now given the gentleness of '*Im Frühling*'. The Andantino is related to '*Pilgerweise*' (D789) of 1823. In the *C minor*, the theme of the Menuetto mimics the Presto vivace of an early quartet, D18: the first movement draws material from its contemporaries '*Kriegers Ahnung*' and '*Der Atlas*' (D957).

More puzzling still is the opening of Schubert's 1814 setting of the cathedral scene from '*Faust*' (D126), which reappears in the bass line for the first movement development of the *B flat Sonata*. In the Goethe setting, Gretchen is taunted by the Devil to the strains of a *Dies Irae*; and the main theme of the sonata's *Molto moderato* quotes a second episode in which the choir sings '*Quid sum miser tum dicturus.*' The significance of these clandestine codes is unknown, but their presence surely contributes to the trilogy's status as a summation of Schubert's work.

Above all, the D958 sonata serves as a quarry of material to be used throughout its successors. The little motif of a sixth and its descending scale we have already noticed: it crops up again in the *B flat Sonata*, and in both the Andantino and Scherzo of the A major, where it adds to a sense of family kinship, ambivalence, and ultimately bliss. Many other bonds – including a use of chromaticism more audacious and questioning even than Mozart's – alternately pull the three together, and wrench them apart. Most memorable are the simple bass octaves of the A major and B flat: at first a proud call-to-arms, then something as fine as a delicately plucked cello, and at last (in the slow movement of D960) as the heart of music that draws us to the still point of a turning world. One realizes that Schubert then has no need of harmonic movement, or dynamism of any kind. He floats like a diver through an almost silent realm, hovering between keys to generate an expectant poise, making the inevitable into something for us to marvel at, as if it had been reborn.

According to Theodore Adorno in an essay written in 1928, Schubert's work is a landscape. It is an arena not for the ostentatious triumph of reason but for the interplay of forces on their own terms, viewed from their own perspectives. Comparison between Schubert's sketches and his first drafts for these sonatas reveals a change in his perception of musical space. The music begins to breathe, details start to tell, minutiae achieve the suspense and scale of immensities. The sonata becomes a work of self-realization, in which free imagining allows each impulse to find its own shape and motives. This inspired the essayist Dieter Schnebel to speak of a 'search for liberated time'. Time is dream-like, giving room moment by moment to wildly differing frames of reference, without the need for conclusive catharsis.

To Schubert the trilogy represented his 'three great sonatas', as if to disown everything that had gone before. Schumann was nonplussed by them, and especially by the last, which had been dedicated to him after its composer's death by Diabelli. He finds it:

> . . . *remarkable enough, impressive in a different way from his others, by virtue of a much greater simplicity of invention (where elsewhere he makes such high demands) and by the spinning out of certain general musical ideas, instead of linking episode to episode with new threads, as he does elsewhere. Thus it ripples along from side to side, always lyrical, never at a loss for what is to come next, as if it could never come to an end. Here and there the even flow is broken by occasional spasms of a more violent kind, which pass quickly, however.*
>
> *If my imagination seems, in this assessment, to be coloured by the idea of his illness, I must leave the matter to calmer judgment.*

Well, the D960 *Sonata* is to music what *The Tempest* is to drama. It is the most wonderful and the most tantalizing piece that Schubert wrote. It is a cipher written upon glass, with something of glass's prismatic quality; a shining eloquence which seems at the same time direct, fickle and unfathomable, capable of assuming whatever significance a virtuoso might impose upon it. Its Andante sostenuto has the luminous quality of a waking dream, which it shares with the Adagio of the *C major Quintet* : composure within weightless stillness, as if a seamless yet infinitely mutable line of awareness were somehow able to glide through an atmosphere of suspended half-light. The mercurial Scherzo is conceived as a series of dialogues, teasing and supremely adroit: the finale measures itself against Beethoven's *Große Fuge*. Here, and only here, is there pathos: the major key struggles to assert itself again and again, storms descend out of silence, only to disperse with the evanescence of Titania's moonbeams. Developments spark into unexpected keys, embark on capricious journeys; at last, within the space of a page, all is made good. I cannot beat Tovey: 'Schubert's tonality is as wonderful as star-clusters, and a verbal description of it is as dull as astronomical tables.' No composer was ever more intimate, or more remote, than this.

Schubert came to the sonatas fresh from his chamber masterpiece, the D956 *Quintet*. 'It is,' remarked Thomas Mann, 'the music one should listen to on one's deathbed' and indeed, it is something rich and strange. Schubert knew that, with Beethoven's death, there was an inheritance to be gained, and he forges a structure of such splendour that it takes the known boundaries of a genre and shakes them apart.

The addition of an extra cello (not the customary viola) darkens its tonal palette and permits melting dialogues, confidences seemingly charged with the calm power of the night. Rarely has the key of C major, emblem for the Enlightenment of magnificent certitude, been so richly compromised or made so fertile in its overtones. A wavering opening chord is instantly questioned: it falls within a few phrases into D minor, yet for the second subject a glide of a major third (from G to E flat) opens up a new horizon of voluptuous ease. Schubert's command of juxtaposed light and shade is at its most compelling. The quintet is a work of burgeoning vitality, where expectation, ambivalence and almost ruthless formal mastery are played off against each other with a daunting economy of gesture.

Its slow movement is about transfigured and luminous memory, unfolding at the pace of a human heart: a consciousness which itself lies beyond emotion, in which the fragments of remembered emotion skim past with the ephemerality of shredded cloud. At the movement's close the vast harmonic space between its two key centres (E flat, and the F minor of an anguished inner episode) is distilled into two bars, and resolved.

The Scherzo pits a boisterous hunting theme against a phantasm that is as chillingly aloof as anything from *Winterreise*. In the finale, the grotesque is the veil of a suave deception: for Schubert takes the affability of Viennese salon music, gives it Beethovenian cut-and-thrust, and ends with violent defiance in the minor. The consequence is a challenge to us which demands new meaning, as the grotesque always is; and as ever with Schubert, the illusion of sunshine is more telling because its origins lie in an awareness of the dark.

SCHUBERT'S DEATH

Weeks after giving the first performance of his final piano sonatas, Schubert was dead. His old headaches had been back, but he was brimming with plans. Impressed by an edition of Handel, he decided to strengthen his grasp of counterpoint and visited a famous teacher, Simon Sechter. He was sketching a *Tenth Symphony*, whose slow movement anticipates the sound-world of Mahler's *Ninth*. He had no idea that anything might be amiss.

Only those things he had learnt to live with. In October he was too queasy to visit Budapest for a concert of his songs. At the end of the month he visited his old haunt, the Rotes Kreuz tavern, and became sick: it was as if the fish had been poisoned. On 12 November he wrote from his bed in Ferdinand's cramped flat,

> *Dear Schober,*
> *I am ill. I have had nothing to eat or drink for five days now, and can only wander feebly and uncertainly between my armchair and bed. Rinna is treating me. If I take any food, I bring it up. Please be so good, then, as to come to my aid in this desperate condition with something to read. I have read Cooper's* The Last of the Mohicans, The Spy, The Pilot *and* The Pioneers.

It was his final letter. By 17 November he was delirious, violently so the following day. He was unconscious the day after until three in the afternoon, when he turned his head to the wall and whispered, 'Here, here is my end.'

On 21 November, Schubert's body was carried to St Joseph's Church in the Margareten. It was a respectably well-attended funeral, despite the drizzle: and it was Second Class, the best his family could afford. Sechter provided a fugue. The choir sang Schubert's '*Pax Vobiscum*', and the bier was carried to the Währing Cemetery where his coffin was lowered into the grave. His wish to be buried near Beethoven had been honoured.

As a man, Schubert disappointed many people who sought him out in order to venerate, like the young miller, a fantasy of their own imagining. Those who knew him spoke of a modest, reticent, gently humorous nature, only truly at ease among friends, and awkward or blunt with strangers. Mayrhofer was characteristically forthright: 'His character was a mixture of tenderness and coarseness, sensuality and candour, sociability and melancholy'. Friends asked to describe his appearance compared him to a drunken cabby with tobacco-stained teeth. He died at 31, the age by which Beethoven and Mahler had finished their first symphonies.

Grillparzer, asked for an epitaph, responded that 'he bade poetry sing and music speak.' The inscription eventually chosen to be carved on Schubert's tomb reads:

> *The Art of Music Here Entombed a Rich Possession*
> *But Even Fairer Hopes.*

SCHUBERT'S MISSION

With his mother's death on 28 May 1812, Schubert's composing came to a halt. A month later, he began the frenetic activity which lasted until the end of his life. In Freudian terms, her removal from the living delivered him from female temptation. Her death and his flight became equivalent events: the years of exile standing for social annihilation, the grave for mother's bed, and both images woven (as in Ernest Jones's 1951 analysis of 'dying together') into 'a voyage of discovery, as a journey to a land where hidden things will be revealed.'

Schubert in his last year said, 'It sometimes seems to me as if I did not belong to this world at all.' Both as an artist and a man, he treasured his singularity, his creativity, his divergence from a stifling and obscurantist official culture. In November 1822, he inscribed Goethe's words in the album of a friend:

One thing will not do for all
Let each live in his tradition
Each consider his own mission,
And who stands, beware a fall.

'Give me your hand' says Death in '*Der Tod und das Mädchen*'. 'I am a friend, and I do not come to punish you.' Schubert is an inhabitant of that 'gloomy shore' where, writes the poet of Gruppe aus dem Tartarus: ' . . . neither sun nor stars shine, where no song is heard, where no friend is to be found. Oblivion breathes an air of peace that is heavy with death.'

'It seems' proposes Einstein, 'as if a poem of this kind was the direct result of a conversation between Schubert and his friends, and had immediately been set to music by him.'

His creative animus is, as much as his parable, penetrated by pain and love. His lifelong rebellion against the circle 'in which youths and old men perpetually walk' is tempered by his need for a brotherhood to whom he can belong, even submit, on the long road towards knowledge and the void beyond. Schubert was a misfit in his own society, who yearned for an era when his mother was still alive and emotion was clean. 'His music', to quote Solomon once more, 'is his defence of beauty against the wasting effects of reality.'

SCHUBERT'S POSTHUMOUS REPUTATION

Six months after the funeral, the Vienna correspondent of the (London) *Harmonicon* found space to report:

> *Franz Schubert, the talented and well-known composer, lately died. . . . As proof of his industry, and of the hopes he had formed of acquiring renown in the different departments of his art, we may mention that among his papers were found twelve grand operas, five operettas, eight masses, ten symphonies, besides several sonatas, quatuors, and above two hundred songs. On the occasion of his funeral a new Requiem by Anselm Hütten-brenner was produced, the music of which is full of striking effects: the mournful impact of the words and the liveliness of the sounds are at open war with each other.*

The inventory of Schubert's effects was more commonplace:

3 cloth coats, 3 frock coats, 10 pairs of trousers, 9 waistcoats,
1 hat, 5 pairs of shoes, 2 pairs of boots, 4 shirts, 6 neckerchiefs
and pocket handkerchiefs. 13 pairs of socks, 1 sheet, 2 blankets,
1 mattress, 1 featherbed cover, 1 counterpane. Apart from some
old music . . . no belongings of the deceased are to be found.

His loyal, mundane friends, dimly conscious that they had lost
something greater than they could have known, began the process
of elaboration that would elevate Schubert's companionship into
a fairy-tale, replete with love-stricken sighs and fanciful meetings
with Beethoven. The public was harder to convince. Almost five
hundred of his compositions had been published, and he had
earned from them as much as a telephonist might earn today in
one year.

Schubert's lowly origins, the humiliations he had suffered
from his youth, the shame of constant rejection and needy circumstances, his lack of instrumental virtuosity: these contrib-
uted to a gaucheness that inhibited him in any enterprise. He
had sold Diabelli a group of compositions for 300 florins or less
for the set, only for Ignaz Sonnleithner to prove that a shrewd
salesman could – on his behalf – command 200 florins and more
apiece. If any person's worth is measured by the money he
expects, Schubert gave Vienna the verdict it could use against
him. The music of the Schubertiads had too rarely penetrated
beyond a closed circle, and it was left to those who had heard it
there to plead the composer's case after his death. Already manuscripts were hopelessly scattered.

Ferdinand promoted his brother's work indefatigably: adver-
tising for lost cantatas, contacting those composers amongst
whom rumours of Schubert's gift was beginning to spread. Liszt
acclaimed Schubert as 'the most poetic musician who has lived'
and did his best to help, playing eloquent transcriptions of
unknown songs to his Society audiences.

The turning point for non-vocal music came on New Year's
Day 1839, when Schumann saw the contents of a polished black
chest. 'The riches that lay here piled up made me tremble with
pleasure. Where to begin, where to stop?' Within were Schubert's
surviving manuscripts, and Schumann grasped the autograph of
the *'Great' Symphony in C.* 'How refreshing is this feeling of
overflowing wealth! With others we always tremble for the con-

clusion and we are troubled lest we find ourselves disappointed.' But this? 'It transports us into a world where I cannot recall ever having been before.'

At first, the violinists of the Leipzig Gewandhaus orchestra baulked at their role as accompanists to the woodwind in the symphony's finale, but Mendelssohn persevered and conducted its premiere, in a shortened version, on 29 March. The Vienna Philharmonic played two movements only, and in 1844, the London Philharmonic Society laughed it out of court. Elsewhere opinions were changing.

Throughout the nineteenth century, Europe and New York witnessed a spate of discoveries. In 1839 *The Musical World* in London, commented: ' All Paris has been in a state of amazement at the posthumous diligence of the song-writer F. Schubert'. As late as 1862 Brahms's colleague Eduard Hanslick wrote in Vienna, 'The master has been dead for thirty years, and yet it is as if he continued to work invisibly – one can hardly keep up with him.' The *Octet* and several quartets were about to be performed for the first time. In 1883 a collected edition of Schubert's music appeared, and in 1885 Brahms (having worked doggedly as editor of the symphonies) urged a young Richard Strauss to study Schubert's dances.

Sixty years later, during *Metamorphosen*, Strauss acknowledged a debt in his sketch book: 'Lucky Schubert, who could compose what he wanted, whatever his genius made him do.' It was to the word an echo of Salieri's verdict when, in 1821, he had seen the rough draft of '*Gretchen*'.

The rest has been a matter of time. Schubert's songs became favourites in the earliest days of the gramophone, and the vintage performances of Elisabeth Schumann – hiss, crackles, warts and all – celebrate a level of spontaneity from which glossy sopranos still have a daunting amount to learn. Pablo Casals knew Schubert was special for him, and to celebrate the centenary in 1928 he embarked on the symphonies with his orchestra in Barcelona.

In 1941 Toscanini conducted a Philadelphia performance of the '*Great*' *C major*, which the critic Spike Hughes described as 'legendary' in its confidence, its inevitability and effervescing excitement. It was left to Artur Schnabel and Thomas Beecham to champion the piano sonatas and early symphonies through records and broadcasts. This takes us beyond 1945.

John Reed has described Schubert's distinction in terms of its felicity:

> *Schubert himself once wrote a song called* 'Seligkeit' ('Happiness', D433), *a gay and unsophisticated little piece untroubled by thoughts of time and change. Felicity conveys much more than this; it is happiness muted by the sense of inevitable loss, of a harmony still within reach of our imagination, like the image of ancient rites on a Greek vase.*

All this is true, yet it is in danger of reducing a robust and urgent force to nostalgia. Like Beethoven, Schubert recognized in himself 'the most miserable of men', and he was right to perceive his life as that of a nomad in a private domain. Yet it was a prospect that in his last year had sights set resolutely on the future.

In his own appraisal Alfred Einstein speaks of a composer who follows:

> *... unreservedly and without heed a single impulse – to create; and who in his music finds – partly of his own free will and partly out of sheer necessity – the only means of meeting the challenge of human existence. But he is not a typical Romantic like all the other composers who came into the world during the twenty years which followed his birth. He is without spiritual discord; he still has the courage to express the full sensuousness and richness of life. He is a Romantic Classicist and belongs in the great company of Haydn, Mozart and Beethoven. He left no successors. The feeling that he inspires in later ages is an infinite longing for a lost paradise of purity, spontaneity and innocence.*

A euphoric tribute, and it misses the self-analysis that underpins this passionate conviction of a creative voice. Grasp that, and you have what makes Schubert our contemporary. If knowledge is the mirror that makes us human, if art provides the reflexiveness that makes possible our changing conception of self, the vision Schubert has for us remains uniquely compelling, far-reaching and humane.

SELECTED FURTHER READING

There are hundreds of books and articles on Schubert, but these are some of the best. The easiest introduction is Maurice Brown's. Capell and Einstein are classics which have not lost their special insights over the years, while *19th Century Music* (a scholarly journal, but often accessible) gives a taste of the latest thinking in Schubert research.

Maurice J.E. Brown: *The New Grove Schubert* (Macmillan, 1982)

Richard Capell: *Schubert's Songs* (Gerald Duckworth, revised edition 1957)

Edited by Otto Erich Deutsch: *Schubert: Memoirs by his Friends* (Adam and Charles Black, 1958)

Alfred Einstein: *Schubert: the Man and his Music* (Cassell, 1951)

Edited by Walter Frisch: *Schubert: Critical and Analytical Studies* (University of Nebraska Press, 1986)

Franz Gal: *Schubert and the Essence of Melody* (Victor Gollancz, 1974)

George Marek: *Schubert* (Robert Hale, 1986)

Brian Newbould: *Schubert and the Symphony: A New Perspective* (Toccata Press, 1992)

Charles Osborne: *Schubert and his Vienna* (Weidenfeld and Nicholson, 1985)

Philip Radcliffe: *Schubert Piano Sonatas* (BBC Music Guides, 1967)

John Reed: *Schubert: The Final Years* (Faber and Faber, 1972)

J.A. Westrup: *Schubert Chamber Music* (BBC Music Guides, 1969)

Translated by Richard Wigmore: *Schubert: The Complete Song Texts* (Victor Gollancz, 1992)

University of California: *19th Century Music* 1977 onwards (academic periodical and source of many articles by Solomon, Youens, Cone, Kramer and others: some of them reproduced in Frisch)

COMPLETE LIST OF WORKS

This list follows Otto Eric Deutsch's *Schubert: Thematic Catalogue of All His Works in Chronological Order* (1951, 1979), which introduced the modern Deutsch (D) numbers. The works, arranged into categories, are ordered thus: **D number**, *name of work* or *song-title* plus poet (in parentheses), and year of composition.

SONGS

D1a, 'Song sketch' (no text), 1810; D5, 'Hagars Klage' (Schückling), 1811; D6, 'Des Mädchens Klage' (1) (Schiller), 1811; D7, 'Leichenfantaise' (Schiller), 1811; D10, 'Des Vatermörder' (Pfeffel), 1811; D15, 'Der Geistertanz' (Matthisson), 1812; D17, 'Quell' innocente figlio' (Metastasio), 1812; D23, 'Klaglied' (Rochlitz), 1812; D30, 'Der Jüngling am Bache' (Schiller), 1812; D33, 'Entra l'uomo allor che nasce' (Metastasio), 1812; D35, 'Serbate, o dei custodi' (3) (Metastasio), 1812; D39, 'Lebenstraum' (Baumberg), 1810; D42, 'Misero Pargoletto' (Metastasio), 1813; D44, 'Totengräberlied' (Hölty), 1813

D50, 'Die Schatten' (Matthisson), 1813; D52, 'Sehnsucht' (Schiller), 1813; D59, 'Verklärung' (Pope), 1813; D73, 'Thekla: eine Geisterstimme' (Schiller), 1813; D76, 'Pensa, che questo istante' (Metastasio), 1813; D77, 'Der Taucher' (Schiller), 1813–14; D78, 'Son fra l'onde' (Metastasio), 1813; D81, 'Auf den Sieg der Deutschen' (?Schubert), 1813; D83, 'Zur Namensfeier des Herrn Andras Siller' (unknown), 1813; D93, 'Don Gayseros' (de la Motte), 1815; D95, 'Adelaide' (Matthisson), 1814; D97, 'Trost: an Elisa' (Matthisson), 1814; D98, 'Errinerungen' (1) (Matthisson), 1814; D99, 'Andenken' (Matthisson), 1814

D100, 'Geisternähe' (Matthisson), 1814; D101, 'Errinerung' (Matthisson), 1814; D102, 'Die Betende' (Matthisson), 1814; D104, 'Die Befreier Europas in Paris' (Mikan), 1814; D107, 'Lied aus der Ferne' (Matthisson), 1814; D108, 'Der Abend' (Matthisson), 1814; D109, 'Lied der Liebe' (Matthisson), 1814; D111, 'Der Taucher' (Schiller), 1814; D113, 'An Emma' (Schiller), 1814; D114, 'Romanze' (Matthisson), 1814; D115, 'An Laura, als sie Klopstocks' (Matthisson), 1814; D116, 'Der Geistertanz' (Matthisson), 1814; D117, 'Das Mädchen aus der Fremde' (Schiller), 1814; D118, 'Gretchen am Spinnrade' (Goethe), 1814; D119, 'Nachtgesang' (Goethe), 1814; D120, 'Trost in Tränen' (Goethe), 1814; D121, 'Schäfers Klagelied' (Goethe), 1814; D122, 'Ammenlied' (Lubi), 1814; D123, 'Sehnsucht' (Goethe), 1814; D124, 'Am See' (Mayrhofer), 1814

D126, 'Szene aus Goethes Faust' (Goethe), 1814; D134, 'Ballade' (J. Kenner), 1815; D138, 'Rastlose Liebe' (Goethe), 1815; D141, 'Der Mondabend' (Kumpf), 1815; D142, 'Geistes-Gruss' (Goethe), 1815; D143, 'Genügsamkeit' (Schober), 1815; D144, 'Romanze' (Stolberg), 1816; D149, 'Der Sänger' (Goethe), 1815

D150, 'Lodas Gespenst' (Ossian), 1816; D151, 'Auf einen Krichhof' (Schlechta), 1815; D152, 'Minona' (Bertrand), 1815; D153, 'Als ich sie erröten sah' (Ehrlich), 1815; D153, 'Das Bild' (unknown), 1815; D159, 'Die

Erwartung' (Schiller), 1816; **D160**, *'Am Flusse'* (Goethe), 1815; **D161**, *'Am Mignon'* (Goethe), 1815; **D162**, *'Nähe des Geliebten'* (Goethe), 1815; **D163**, *'Sängers Morgenlied'* (Körner), 1815; **D164**, *'Liebesrausch'* (Körner), 1815; **D165**, *'Sängers Morgenlied'* (Körner), 1815; **D166**, *'Amphiaraos'* (Körner), 1815; **D169**, *'Trinklied vor der Schlacht'* (Körner), 1815; **D170**, *'Schwertlied'* (Körner), 1815; **D172**, *'Der Morgenstern'* (Körner), 1815; **D174**, *'Das war ich'* (Körner), 1815

D176, *'Die Sterne'* (Fellinger), 1815; **D177**, *'Vergebliche Liebe'* (Bernard), 1815; **D179**, *'Liebesrausch'* (Körner), 1815; **D180**, *'Sehnsucht der Liebe'* (Körner), 1815; **D182**, *'Die erste Liebe'* (Fellinger), 1815; **D183**, *'Trinklied'*, with chorus (Zettler), 1815; **D186**, *'Die Sterbende'* (Matthisson), 1815; **D187**, *'Stimme der Liebe'* (Matthisson), 1815; **D188**, *'Naturgenuss'* (Matthisson), 1815; **D189**, *'An die Freude'*, with chorus (Schiller), 1815; **D191**, *'Des Mädchens Klage'* (Schiller), 1815; **D192**, *'Der Jüngling am Bache'* (Schiller), 1815; **D193**, *'An den Mond'* (Hölty), 1815; **D194**, *'Die Mainacht'* (Hölty), 1815; **D195**, *'Amalia'* (Schiller), 1815; **D196**, *'An die Nachtigall'* (Hölty), 1815; **D197**, *'An die Apfelbäume'* (Hölty), 1815; **D198**, *'Seufzer'* (Hölty), 1815

D201, *'Auf den Tod einer Nachtigall'* (Hölty), 1815; **D204**, *'Das Traumbild'* (lost), 1815; **D206**, *'Liebeständelei'* (Körner), 1815; **D207**, *'Der Liebende'* (Hölty), 1815; **D208**, *'Die Nonne'* (Hölty), 1815; **D209**, *'Der Liedler'* (Kenner), 1815; **D210**, *'Die Liebe'* (Goethe), 1815; **D211**, *'Adelwold und Emma'* (Bertrand), 1815; **D212**, *'Die Nonne'* (obsolete D no.) (Hölty), 1815; **D213**, *'Der Traum'* (Hölty), 1815; **D214**, *'Die Laube'* (Hölty), 1815; **D215a**, *'Meerestille'* (1) (Goethe), 1815;

D216, *'Meerestille'* (2) (Goethe), 1815; **D217**, *'Kolmas Klage'* (Ossian), 1815; **D218**, *'Grablied'* (Kenner), 1815; **D219**, *'Das Finden'* (Kosegarten), 1815; **D221**, *'Der Abend'* (Hölty), 1815; **D222**, *'Lieb Minna'* (Stadler), 1815; **D224**, *'Wandrers Nachtlied'* (Goethe), 1815

D225, *'Der Fischer'* (Goethe), 1815; **D226**, *'Werster Verlust'* (Goethe), 1815; **D227**, *'Idens Nachtgesang'* (Kosegarten), 1815; **D228**, *'Von Ida'* (Kosegarten), 1815; **D229**, *'Die Erscheinung'* (Kosegarten), 1815; **D230**, *'Der Täuschung'* (Kosegarten), 1815; **D231**, *'Das Sehnen'* (Kosegarten), 1815; **D233**, *'Geist der Liebe'* (Kosegarten), 1815; **D234**, *'Tischlied'* (Goethe), 1815; **D235**, *'Abends unter der Linde'* (1) (Kosegarten), 1815; **D237**, *'Abends unter der Linde'* (2) (Kosegarten), 1815; **D238**, *'Die Mondnacht'* (Kosegarten), 1815; **D240**, *'Huldigung'* (Kosegarten), 1815; **D241**, *'Alles um Liebe'* (Kosegarten), 1815; **D245**, *'An den Frühling'* (Schiller), 1815; **D246**, *'Die Bürgeschaft'* (Schiller), 1815; **D247**, *'Die Spinnerin'* (Goethe), 1815; **D248**, *'Lob des Tokayers'* (Baumberg), 1815

D250, *'Das Geheimnis'* (Schiller), 1815; **D251**, *'Hoffnung'* (Schiller), 1815; **D252**, *'Das Mädchen aus dem Fremde'* (Schiller), 1815; **D253**, *'Punschlied: im Norden zu singen'* (Schiller), 1815; **D254**, *'Der Gott und der Bajadere'* (Goethe), 1815; **D255**, *'Der Rattenfänger'* (Goethe), 1815; **D256**, *'Der Schatzgräber'* (Goethe), 1815; **D257**, *'Heidenröslein'* (Goethe), 1815; **D258**, *'Bundeslied'* (Goethe), 1815; **D259**, *'An den Mond'* (Goethe), 1815; **D260**, *'Wonne der Wehmut'* (Goethe), 1815; **D261**, *'Wer kauft Liebesgötter?'* (Goethe), 1815; **D262**, *'Die Fröhlichkeit'* (Prandstetter), 1815; **D263**, *'Cora an die Sonne'* (Baumberg), 1815; **D264**, *'Der Morgenkuss'* (Baumberg), 1815; **D265**,

'*Abendständchen: An Lina*' (Baumberg), 1815; **D266**, '*Morgenlied*' (Stolberg), 1815; **D270**, '*an die Sonne*' (Baumberg), 1815; **D271**, '*Der Weiberfreund*' (Cowley), 1815; **D272**, '*An die Sonne*' (Tiedge), 1815; **D273**, '*Lilla an die Morgenröte*' (unknown), 1815; **D274**, '*Tischerlied*' (unknown), 1815

D275, '*Totenkranz für ein Kind*' (Matthisson), 1815; **D276**, '*Abendlied*' (Stolberg), 1815; **D278**, '*Ossians Lied*' (Ossian), 1815; **D280**, '*Das Rosenband*' (Klopstock), 1815; **D281**, '*Das Mädchen von Inistore*' (Ossian), 1815; **D282**, '*Cronnan*' (Ossian), 1815; **D283**, '*An die Frühling*' (Schiller), 1815; **D284**, '*Lied*' (?Schiller), 1815; **D285**, '*Furcht der Geliebten*' (Klopstock), 1815; **D286**, '*Selma und Selmar*' (Klopstock), 1815; **D287**, '*Vaterlandslied*' (Klopstock), 1815; **D288**, '*An Sie*' (Klopstock), 1815; **D289**, '*Die Sommernacht*' (Klopstock), 1815; **D290**, '*Die frühen Gräber*' (Klopstock), 1815; **D291**, '*Dem Unendlichen*' (Klopstock), 1815; **D292**, '*Klage*' (see D371), 1815; **D293**, '*Shilric und Vinvela*' (Ossian), 1815; **D295**, '*Hoffnung*' (Goethe), 1815; **D296**, '*An den Mond*' (Goethe), ?1816; **D297**, '*Augenlied*' (Mayrhofer), ?1817; **D298**, '*Liane*' (Mayrhofer), 1815

D300, '*Der Jüngling an der Quelle*' (Salis-Seewis), 1815; **D301**, '*Lambertine*' (Stoll), 1815; **D302**, '*Labetrank der Liebe*' (Stoll), 1815; **D303**, '*An die Geliebte*' (Stoll), 1815; **D304**, '*Wiegenlied*' (Körner), 1815; **D305**, '*Mein Gruss an den Mai*' (Kumpf), 1815; **D306**, '*Skolie*' (Deinhardstein), 1815; **D307**, '*Die Sternewelten*' (Jarnik), 1815; **D308**, '*Die Macht der Liebe*' (Kalchberg), 1815; **D309**, '*Das gestörte Glück*' (Körner), 1815; **D310**, '*Sehnsucht*' (Goethe), 1815; **D311**, '*An den Mond*' (unknown), 1815; **D312**,

'*Hektors Abschied*' (Schiller), 1815; **D313**, '*Die Sterne*' (Kosegarten), 1815; **D314**, '*Nachtgesang*' (Kosegarten), 1815; **D315**, '*An Rosa 1*' (Kosegarten), 1815; **D316**, '*An Rosa 2*' (Kosegarten), 1815; **D317**, '*Idens Schwanenlied*' (Kosegarten), 1815; **D318**, '*Schwanengesang*' (Kosegarten), 1815; **D319**, '*Luisens Antwort*' (Kosegarten), 1815; **D320**, '*Der Zufriedene*' (Reissig), 1815; **D321**, '*Mignon*' (Goethe), 1815; **D322**, '*Mignon*' (Goethe), 1815; **D323**, '*Klage der Ceres*' (Schiller), 1815; **D325**, '*Harfenspieler*' (Goethe), 1815

D327, '*Lorma (1)*' (Ossian), 1815; **D328**, '*Erlkönig*' (Goethe), 1815; **D329**, '*Die drei Sänger*' (Bobrik), 1815; **D330**, '*Das Grab*' (Salis-Seewis), 1815; **D342**, '*An mein Klavier*' (Schubart), 1816; **D343**, '*Am Tage aller Seelen*' (Jacobi), 1816; **D344**, '*Am ersten Maimorgen*' (Claudius), 1816; **D350**, '*Der Entfernten*' (2) (Salis-Seewis), 1816; **D351**, '*Fischerlied*' (1), Salis-Seewis, 1816

D352, '*Licht und Liebe*' (Collin), 1816; **D358**, '*Die Nacht*' (Uz), 1816; **D359**, '*Sehnsucht*' (Goethe), 1816; **D360**, '*Lied eines Schiffers an die Dioskuren*' (Mayrhofer), 1816; **D361**, '*Am Bach im Frühlinge*' (Schober), 1816; **D362**, '*Zufriedenheit*' (Claudius), 1816; **D363**, '*An Chloen*' (Uz), 1816; **D367**, '*Der König in Thule*' (Goethe), 1816; **D368**, '*Jägers Abendlied*' (Goethe), 1816; **D369**, '*An Schwager Kronos*' (Goethe), 1816; **D371**, '*Klage*' (unknown), 1816; **D372**, '*An die Natur*' (Stolberg-Stolberg), 1816; **D373**, '*Lied*' (Fourqué), 1816; **D375**, '*Der Tod Oskars*' (Ossian), 1816

D376, '*Lorma*' (2) (Ossian), 1816; **D381**, '*Morgenlied*' (unknown), 1816; **D382**, '*Abendlied*' (unknown), 1816; **D388**, '*Laura am Klavier*' (Schiller), 1816; **D389**, '*Des Mädchens Klage*' (Schiller), 1816;

D390, '*Entzückung an Laura*' (Schiller), 1816; D391, '*Die vier Weltalter*' (Schiller), 1816; D392, '*Pflügerlied*' (Salis-Seewis), 1816; D393, '*Die Einsiedelei*' (2) (Salis-Seewis), 1816; D394, '*An die Harmonie*' (Salis-Seewis), 1816; D395, '*Lebensmelodien*' (Schlegel), 1816; D396, '*Gruppe aus dem Tartarus*' (Schiller), 1816; D397, '*Ritter Toggenburg*' (Schiller), 1816; D398, '*Frühlingslied*' (Hölty), 1816; D399, '*Auf den Tod einer Nachtigall*' (2) (Hölty), 1816

D400, '*Die Knabenzeit*' (Hölty), 1816; D401, '*Winterlied*' (Hölty), 1816; D402, '*Der Flüchtling*' (Schiller), 1816; D403, '*Lied*' (Salis-Seewis), 1816; D404, '*Die Herbstnacht*' (Salis-Seewis), 1816; D405, '*Der Herbstabend*' (Salis-Seewis), 1816; D406, '*Abschied von der Harfe*' (Salis-Seewis), 1816; D409, '*Der verfehlte Stunde*' (Schlegel), 1816; D410, '*Sprache der Liebe*' (Schlegel), 1816; D411, '*Daphne der Bache*' (Stolberg-Stolberg), 1816; D412, '*Stimme der Liebe*' (Stolberg-Stolberg), 1816; D413, '*Entzückung*' (Matthisson), 1816; D414, '*Geist der Liebe*' (Matthisson), 1816; D415, '*Klage*' (Matthisson), 1816; D416, '*Lied in der Abswesenheit*' (Stolberg-Stolberg), 1816; D418, '*Stimme der Liebe*' (Matthisson), 1816; D419, '*Julius an Theone*' (Matthisson), 1816

D429, '*Minnelied*' (Hölty), 1816; D430, '*Die frühe Liebe*' (Hölty), 1816; D431, '*Blumenleid*' (Hölty), 1816; D432, '*Der Leidende*' (Hölty), 1816; D433, '*Seligkeit*' (Hölty), 1816; D434, '*Ertelied*' (Hölty), 1816; D436, '*Klage*' (Hölty), 1816; D437, '*Klage*' (obsolete D no.) (Hölty), 1816; D442, '*Das grosse Halleluja*' (Klopstock), 1816; D443, '*Schlachtlied*' (Klopstock), 1816; D444, '*Die Gestirne*' (Klopstock), 1816; D445, '*Edone*'

(Klopstock), 1816; D446, '*Die Leibesgötter*' (Uz), 1816; D447, '*An den Schlaf*' (unknown), 1816; D448, '*Gott im Frülinge*'[sic] (Uz), 1816; D449, '*Der gute Hirt*' (Uz), 1816; D450, '*Fragment aus dem Aeschylus*' (Aeschylus), 1816

D454, '*Grablied auf einem Soldaten*' (Schubart), 1816; D455, '*Freunde der Kinderjahre*' (Köpkjen), 1816; D456, '*Das Heimweh*' (Winkler), 1816; D457, '*An die untergehende Sonne*' (Kosegarten), 1816; D458, '*Aus Diego Manazares*' (Schlechta), 1816; D462, '*An Chloen*' (Jacobi), 1816; D463, '*Hochzeit-Lied*' (Jacobi), 1816; D464, '*In der Mitternacht*' (Jacobi), 1816; D465, '*Trauer der Liebe*' (Jacobi), 1816; D466, '*Die Perle*' (Jacobi), 1816; D467, '*Pflicht und Liebe*' (Gotter), 1816; D468, '*An dem Mond*' (Hölty), 1816; D469, '*Mignon*' (Goethe), 1816; D473, '*Liedesend*' (Mayrhofer), 1816; D474, '*Lied des Orpheus*' (Jacobi), 1816; D475, '*Abschied*' (Mayrhofer), 1816

D476, '*Rückweg*' (Mayrhofer), 1816; D477, '*Alte Liebe rostet nie*' (Mayrhofer), 1816; D478, '*Harfenspieler* I' (Goethe), 1816; D479, '*Harfenspieler* II' (Goethe), 1816; D480, '*Harfenspieler* III' (Goethe), 1816; D481, '*Sehnsucht*' (Goethe), 1816; D482, '*Der Sänger am Felsen*' (Pichler), 1816; D483, '*Lied*' (Pichler), 1816; D489, '*Der Wanderer*' (Schmidt von Lübeck), 1816; D490, '*Der Hirt*' (Mayrhofer), 1816; D491, '*Geheimnis*' (Mayrhofer), 1816; D492, '*Zum Punsche*' (Mayrhofer), 1816; D493, '*Der Wanderer*' (Schmidt von Lübeck), 1816; D495, '*Abendlied der Fürstin*' (Mayrhofer), 1816; D496, '*Klage um Ali Bey*' (Claudius), 1816; D497, '*An die Nachtigall*' (Claudius), 1816; D498, '*Wiegenlied*' (unknown), 1816; D499, '*Abendlied*' (Claudius), 1816

D500, '*Phidile*' (Claudius), 1816; D501, '*Zufriedenheit*' (Claudius),

1816; **D502**, '*Herbstlied*' (Salis-Seewis), 1816; **D503**, '*Mailied*' (Hölty), 1816; **D504**, '*Am Grabe Anselmos*' (Claudius), 1816; **D507**, '*Skolie*' (Matthisson), 1816; **D508**, '*Lebenslied*' (Matthisson), 1816; **D509**, '*Leiden der Trennung*' (Metastasio), 1816; **D510**, '*Vedi quanto adoro*' (Metastasio), 1816; **D513**, '*Nur wer die Liebe kennt*' (Werner), 1817; **D514**, '*Die abgeblühte Linde*' (Széchényi), 1817; **D515**, '*Der Flug der Zeit*' (Széchényi), 1817; **D516**, '*Sehnsucht*' (Mayrhofer), 1817; **D517**, '*Der Schäfer und der Reiter*' (Fouqué), 1817; D518, '*An den Tod*' (Schubart), 1817; **D519**, '*Die Blumensprache*' (Platner), 1817; **D520**, '*Frohsinn*' (Castelli), 1817; **D521**, '*Jagdlied*' (Werner), 1817; **D522**, '*Die Liebe*' (Leon), 1817; **D523**, '*Trost*' (Mayrhofer), 1817; **D524**, '*Der Alpenjäger*' (Mayrhofer), 1817; **D525**, '*Wie Ulfru fischt*' (Mayrhofer), 1817

D526, '*Fahrt zum Hades*' (Matthisson), 1817; **D527**, '*Schlaflied*' (Matthisson), 1817; **D528**, '*La pastorella al prato*' (Goldoni), 1817; **D530**, '*An eine Quelle*' (Claudius), 1817; **D531**, '*Der Tod und das Mädchen*' (Claudius), 1817; **D532**, '*Das Lied vom Eifen*' (Claudius), 1817; **D534**, '*Die Nacht*' (Ossian), 1817; **D535**, '*Lied*' (with small orchestra) (unknown), 1817; **D536**, '*Der Schiffer*' (Mayrhofer), 1817; **D539**, '*Am Strome*' (Mayrhofer), 1817; **D540**, '*Philoktet*' (Mayrhofer), 1817; **D543**, '*Auf dem See*' (Goethe), 1817; **D544**, '*Ganymed*' (Goethe), 1817; **D545**, '*Der Jüngling und der Tod*' (Spaun), 1817; **D546**, '*Trost im Liede*' (Schober), 1817; **D547**, '*An die Musik*' (Schober), 1817; **D548**, '*Orest auf Tauris*' (Mayrhofer), 1817; **D549**, '*Mahomets Gesang*' (Goethe), 1817; **D550**, '*Die Forelle*' (Schubart), 1817

D551, '*Pax vobiscum*' (Schober),

1817; **D552**, '*Hänflings Liebeswerbung*' (Kind), 1817; **D553**, '*An der Donau*' (Mayrhofer), 1817; **D554**, '*Uraniens Flucht*' (Mayrhofer), 1817; **D555**, '*Song sketch*' (no text), 1817; **D558**, '*Liebhaber in allen Gestalten*' (Goethe), 1817; **D559**, '*Schweizerleid*' (Goethe), 1817; **D560**, '*Der Goldschmiedsgewsell*' (Goethe), 1817; **D561**, '*Nach einem Gewitter*' (Mayrhofer), 1817; **D562**, '*Fischerlied*' (Salis-Seewis), 1817; **D563**, '*Die Einsiedelei*' (Salis-Seewis), 1817; **D564**, '*Gretchen im Zwinger*' (Goethe), 1817; **D569**, '*Das Grab*' (Salis-Seewis), 1817; **D573**, '*Iphigenia*' (Mayrhofer), 1817

D577, '*Entzückung an Laura*' (Schiller), 1817; **D578**, '*Abschied*' (Schubert), 1817; **D579**, '*Der Knabe in der Wiege*' (Ottenwalt), 1817; **D579a**, '*Vollendung*' (Matthisson), 1817; **D579b**, '*Die Erde*' (Matthisson), 1817; **D582**, '*Augenblicke im Elysium*' (unknown), 1817; **D583**, '*Gruppe aus dem Tartarus*' (Schiller), 1817; **D584**, '*Elysium*' (Schiller), 1817; **D585**, '*Atys*' (Matthisson), 1817; **D586**, '*Erlafsee*' (Matthisson), 1817; **D587**, '*An den Frühling*' (Schiller), 1817; **D588**, '*Der Alpenjäger*' (Schiller), 1817; **D594**, '*Der Kampf*' (Schiller), 1817; **D595**, '*Thekla: eine Geisterstimme*' (Schiller), 1817; **D596**, '*Lied eines Kindes*' (unknown), 1817

D611, '*Auf der Riesenkoppe*' (Körner), 1817; **D614**, '*An den Mond in einer Herbstnacht*' (Schreiber), 1817; **D616**, '*Grablied für die Mutter*' (unknown), 1817; **D619**, 'Vocal exercise, figured bass' (unknown), 1817; **D620**, '*Einsamkeit*' (Mayrhofer), 1817; **D622**, '*Der Blumebrief*' (Schreiber), 1817; **D623**, '*Das Marienbild*' (Schreiber), 1817

D626, '*Das Marienbild*' (Schreiber), 1817; **D627**, '*Das Abendrot*' (Schreiber), 1817; **D628**, '*Sonett 1*' (Petrarch), 1817; **D629**, '*Sonett 2*'

(Petrarch), 1817; **D630**, '*Sonett* III' (Petrarch), 1817; **D631**, '*Blanka (Das Mädchen)*' (Schlegel), 1817; **D632**, '*Von Mitleiden Mariä*' (Schlegel), 1817; **D634**, '*Die Berge*' (Schlegel), 1817; **D636**, '*Sehnsucht* ' (Schiller), 1817; **D637**, '*Hoffnung*' (Schiller), 1817; **D638**, '*Der Jüngling am Bache*' (Schiller), 1817; **D639**, '*Widerschein*' (Schlechta), 1817; **D645**, '*Abend* ' (Tieck), 1817; **D646**, '*Der Gebüsche*' (Schlegel), 1817; **D649**, '*Der Wanderer*' (Schlegel), 1817; **D650**, '*Abendbilder*' (Silbert), 1817

D651, '*Himmelsfunken*' (Silbert), 1817; **D652**, '*Das Mädchen*' (Schlegel), 1817; **D653**, '*Bertas Lied in der Nacht* ' (Grillparzer), 1817; **D654**, '*Am die Freunde*' (Mayrhofer), 1817; **D658**, '*Marie*' (Novalis), 1817; **D659**, '*Hymne* I' (Novalis), 1817; **D660**, '*Hymne* II' (Novalis), 1817; **D661**, '*Hymne* III' (Novalis), 1817; **D662**, '*Hymne* IV' (Novalis), 1817; **D663**, '*Der 13 Psalm* ' (trans. Mendelssohn), 1817; **D669**, '*Beim Winde*' (Mayrhofer), 1817; **D670**, '*Die Sternennächte*' (Mayrhofer), 1817; **D671**, '*Trost* ' (Mayrhofer), 1817; **D672**, '*Nachtstück*' (Mayrhofer), 1817; **D673**, '*Die Liebende schreibt* ' (Goethe), 1817; **D674**, '*Prometheus*' (Goethe), 1817

D677, '*Strophe aus Die Götter Griechenlands*' (Schiller), 1817; **D682**, '*Überallen Auber Liebe*' (Mayrhofer), 1820; **D684**, '*Die Sterne*' (Schlegel), 1820; **D685**, '*Morgenlied* ' (Werner), 1820; **D686**, '*Frülingslaube*' (Uhland), 1820; **D687**, '*Nachthymne*' (Novalis), 1820; **D688**, '*Vier Canzonen*' (Vitorelli, Metastasio, Schiller), 1820; **D690**, '*Abendröte*' (Schlegel), 1823; **D691**, '*Die Vögel*' (Schlegel), 1820; **D692**, '*Der Knabe*' (Schlegel), 1820; **D693**, '*Der Fluss*' (Schlegel), 1820; **D694**, '*Der Schiffer*'

(Schlegel), 1820; **D695**, '*Namenstagslied* ' (Stadler), 1820; **D698**, '*Des Fräuleins*' (Schlechta), 1820; **D690**, '*Abendröte*' (Schlegel), 1820; **D691**, '*Die Vögel* ' (Schlegel), 1820; **D692**, '*Der Knabe*' (Schlegel), 1820; **D693**, '*Der Fluss*' (Schlegel), 1820; **D694**, '*Der Schiffer*' (Schlegel), 1820; **D695**, '*Namenstagslied* ' (Stadler), 1820; **D698**, '*Des Fräuleins Liebesslauschen*' (Schlechta), 1820; **D699**, '*Der entsühnte Orest* ' (Mayrhofer), 1820

D700, '*Freiwilliges Versinken*' (Mayrhofer), 1820; **D702**, '*Der Jüngling auf dem Hügel* ' (Hüttenbrenner), 1820; **D707**, '*Der zürneneden Diana*' (Mayrhofer), 1820; **D708**, '*Im Walde*' (Schlegel), 1820; **D711**, '*Lob der Tränen*' (Schlegel), 1818; **D712**, '*Die gefangenen Sänger*' (Schlegel), 1821; **D713**, '*Der Unglückliche*' (Pichler), 1821; **D715**, '*Versunken*' (Goethe), 1821; **D716**, '*Grenzen der Menschheit* ' (Goethe), 1821; **D717**, '*Suleika* II' (Willemer, née Jung), 1821; **D719**, '*Geheimes*' (Goethe), 1821; **D720**, '*Suleika* I' (Willemer, née Jung), 1821; **D721**, '*Mahomets Gesang*' (Goethe), 1821; **D725**, '*Linde Lüfte wehen, Mez*' (unknown), 1821

D726, '*Mignon* I' (Goethe), 1821; **D727**, '*Mignon* II' (Goethe), 1821; **D728**, '*Johanna Sebus*' (Goethe), 1821; **D731**, '*Der Blumen Schmerz*' (Maylath), 1821; **D736**, '*Ihr Grab*' (Engelhardt), 1822; **D737**, '*An die Leier*' (Bruchmann), 1822; **D738**, '*Im Haine*' (Bruchmann), 1822; **D741**, '*Sei mir gegrüsst* ' (Rückert), 1822; **D742**, '*Der Wachtelschlag*' (Sauter), 1822; **D743**, '*Selige Welt* ' (Senn), 1822; **D744**, '*Schwanengesang*' (Senn), 1822; **D745**, '*Die Rose*' (Schlegel), 1822; **D746**, '*Am See*' (Bruchmann), 1822; **D749**, '*Herr Josef Spaun, Assessor in Linz*' (Collin), 1822

D751, '*Die Liebe hat gelogen*' (Platen-Hallermünde), 1822; **D752**, '*Nachtviolen*' (Mayrhofer), 1822; **D753**, '*Heliopolis* I' (Mayrhofer),

1822; **D754**, '*Heliopolis* II'
(Mayrhofer), 1822; **D756**, '*Du liebst
mich nicht* ' (Platen-Hallermunde),
1822; **D758**, '*Todesmusik*'
(Schober), 1822; **D761**,
'*Schatzgräbers Begehr*' (Schober),
1822; **D762**, '*Schwestergruss*' (Bruch-
mann), 1822; **D764**, '*Der Musen-
sohn*' (Goethe), 1822; **D765**, '*An die
Entfernte*' (Goethe), 1822; **D766**,
'*Am Flusse*' (Goethe), 1822; **D767**,
'*Wilkommen und Abschied*' (Goethe),
1822; **D768**, '*Wandrers Nachtlied* '
(Goethe), 1824; **D770**, '*Drang in
die Ferne*' (Leitner), 1823; **D771**,
'*Der Zwerg*' (Collin), 1822–23;
D772, '*Wehmut* ' (Collin), 1822–23;
D774, '*Auf dem Wasser zu singen*'
(Stolberg-Stolberg), 1823; **D775**,
'*Dass sie hier gewesen*' (Rückert),
1823

D776, '*Du bist die Ruh* ' (Rück-
ert), 1823; **D777**, '*Lachen und We-
inen*' (Rückert), 1823; **D778**,
'*Greisengesang*' (Rückert), 1823;
D778a, '*Die Wallfahrt* ' (Rückert),
1823; **D785**, '*der zürnende Barde*'
(Bruchmann), 1823; **D786**, '*Viola*'
(Schober), 1823; **D788**, '*Lied* '
(Stolberg-Stolberg), 1823; **D789**,
'*Pilgerweise*' (Schober), 1823;
D792, '*Vergissmeinnicht* ' (Schober),
1823; **D793**, '*Das Geheimnis*'
(Schiller), 1823; **D794**, '*Der Pil-
grim*' (Schiller), 1823; **D795**
(Nos.1–20) '*Die schöne Müllerin*'
(Müller), 1823; **D797**, '*Romanze
zum Drama Rosamunde*' (Chézy),
1823; **D799**, '*Im Abendrot* '
(Lappe), 1824

D800, '*Der Einsame*' (Lappe),
1825; **D801**, '*Dithyrambe*'
(Schiller), by June 1826; **D805**,
'*Der Sieg*' (Mayrhofer), 1824;
D806, '*Abenstern*' (Mayrhofer),
1824; **D807**, '*Auflösung*'
(Mayrhofer), 1824; **D822**, '*Lied eine
Kriegers*' (unknown), 1824; **D827**,
'*Nacht und Träume*' (Collin), by June
1823; **D828**, '*Die junge Nonne*'

(Craigher de Jachelutta), 1825;
D829, '*Abschied* ' (Pratobevera),
1826; **D830**, '*Lied der Anne Lyle*'
(MacDonald), 1825; **D831**, '*Gesang
der Norna*' (Scott), 1825; **D832**, '*Des
Sängers Habe*' (Schlechta), 1825;
D833, '*Der blinde Knabe*' (Cibber),
1825; **D834**, '*Im Walde*' (Schulze),
1825; **D837**, '*Ellens Gesang* I' (Scott),
1825; **D838**, '*Ellens Gesang* II' (Scott),
1825; **D839**, '*Ellens Gesang* III'
(Scott), 1825; **D842**, '*Totengräbers He-
imwehe*' (Craigher), 1825; **D843**,
'*Liedes gefangenen Jägers*' (Scott), 1825;
D846, '*Normans Gesang*' (Scott), 1825

D851, '*Das Heimweh*' (Pyrker),
1825; **D852**, '*Die Allmacht* ' (Pyrker),
1825; **D853**, '*Auf der Bruck*'
(Schulze), 1825; **D854**, '*Fülle der
Liebe*' (Schlegel), 1825; **D855**, '*Wied-
ersehn*' (Schlegel), 1825; **D856**,
'*Abendlied für die Entfernte*' (Schlegel),
1825; **D857**, '*Zwei Szenen aus dem
Schauspiel Lacrimas*' (Schütz), 1825;
D860, '*An mein Herz*' (Schulze),
1825; **D861**, '*Der Liebliche Stern*'
(Schulze), 1825; **D862**, '*Um Mitternacht* ' (Schulze), 1826; **D863**, '*An
Gott* ' (Hohlfeld), by 1827; **D864**,
'*Das Totenhemchen*' (Bauernfeld), after
1824; **D865**, '*Widerspruch*' (Seidl),
1826; **D866**, '*Vier Refrainlieder*'
(Seidl), 1828; **D867**, '*Wiegenlied* '
(Seidl), 1826; **D868**, '*Das Echo*' (Castelli), 1826; **D869**, '*Totengräber-Weise*'
(Schlechta), 1826; **D870**, '*Der Wanderer an den Mond* ' (Seidl), 1826;
D871, '*Das Zügenglöcklein*' (Seidl),
1826; **D874**, '*O Quell, was Stömst du
rasch und wild* ', Schulze, 1826

D876, '*Im Jänner 1817*' (Schulze),
1826; **D877**, '*Gesänge aus Wilhelm Meister*' (Goethe), 1826; **D878**, '*Am Fen-
ster*' (Seidl), 1826; **D879**, '*Sehsnucht* '
(Seidl), 1826; **D880**, '*Im Freien*'
(Seidl), 1826; **D881**, '*Fischerweise*'
(Schlechta), 1826; **D882**, '*Im Frühling*' (Schulze), 1826; **D883**, '*Lebensmut* ' (Schulze), 1826; **D884**,
'*über Wildemann*' (Schulze), 1826;

D888, *'Trinklied'* (Shakespeare), 1826; **D889**, *'Standchen (Hark, hark the lark)'* (Shakespeare), 1826; **D890**, *'Hippolits Lied'* (Gerstenberg), 1826; **D891**, *'Gesang (An Sylvia)'* (Shakespeare), 1826; **D896**, *'Fröhliches Scheiden'* (Leitner), 1827; **D896a**, *'Sie in jedem Liede'* (Leitner), 1827; **D896b**, *'Wolke und Quelle'* (Leitner), 1827

D902, *'Drei Gesange'* (Metastasio), 1827; **D904**, *'Alinde'* (Rochlitz), 1827; **D905**, *'An die Laute'* (Rochlitz), 1827; **D906**, *'Der Vater mit dem Kind'* (Bauernfeld), 1827; **D907**, *'Romanze des Richard Löwenherz'* (Scott), 1827; **D909**, *'Jägers Liebeslied'* (Schober), 1827; **D910**, *'Schiffers Scheidelied'* (Schober), 1827; **D911** (Nos.1–24) *'Winterreise'* (Müller), 1827; **D916a**, *'Song sketch'* (no text), 1827; **D917**, *'Das Lied in Grünen'* (Reil), 1827; **D919**, *'Frühlingslied'* (Pollak), 1827; **D922**, *'Heimliches Lieben'* (Klenke), 1827; **D923**, *'Eine altschottische Ballade'* (anonymous English), 1827

D926, *'Das Weinen'* (Leitner), 1827; **D927**, *'Vor meiner Wiege'* (Leitner), 1827; **D931**, *'Der Wallensteiner Lanznecht beim Trunk'* (Leitner), 1827; **D932**, *'Der Kreuzzug'* (Leitner), 1827; **D933**, *'Des Fischers Liebesglück'* (Leitner), 1827; **D937**, *'Lebensmut'* (Rellstab), 1828; **D938**, *'Der Winterabend'* (Leitner), 1828; **D939**, *'Die Sterne'* (Leitner), 1828; **D943**, *'Auf dem Strom'* (Rellstab), 1828; **D945**, *'Herbt'* (Rellstab), 1828; **D949**, *'Widerschein'* (Schlechta), 1828

D955, *'Glaube, Hoffnung and Liebe'* (Kuffner), 1828; **D957** (Nos.1–14) *'Schwanengesang'* (Rellstab, Heine, Seidl), 1828; **D965**, *'Der Hirt auf dem Felsen'* (Müller), 1828; **D989**, *'Vollendung'* (Matthisson), 1828; **D990**, *'Der Graf von Habsburg'* (Schiller), ?1815; **D990a**, *'Kaiser Maximilian auf der Martinswand'* (Collin) ?1815

FOR MIXED VOICES

D17, *'Quell' innocente figlio'* (Metastasio), 1812; **D33**, *'Entra L'uomo allor che nasce'* (Metastasio), 1812; **D34**, *'Te solo adoro'* (Metastasio), 1812; **D35**, *'Serbate, o dei custodi'* (Metastasio), 1812; **D47**, *'Dithyrambe (Der Besuch)'* (Schiller), 1813; **D168**, *'Nun lasst uns den Leib begraben'* (Klopstock), 1815; **D168a**, *'Osterlied'* (Klopstock), 1815; **D232**, *'Hymne an den Unendlichen'* (Schiller), 1815; **D294**, *'Namensfeier für Franz Michael Vierthaler'* (unknown), 1815; **D329a**, *'Das Grab'* (Salis-Seewis), 1815

D439, *'An die Sonne'* (Uz), 1816; **D440**, *'Chor der Engel'* (Goethe), 1816; **D451**, *'Prometheus'* (Dräxler von Carin), 1816; **D472**, *'Kantate zu Ehren von Josef Spendou'* (Hohseisel), 1816

D609, *'Die Geseligkeit'* (Unger), 1818; **D642**, *'Viel tausend Sterne prangen'* (Eberhard), ?1812; **D643a**, *'Das Grab'* (Salis-Seewis), 1819; **D665**, *'Im traulichen Kreise'* (Unger), 1818; **D666**, *'Kantate zum Geburtstag des Sängers Johann Michael Vogl'* (Stadler), 1819; **D689**, *'Lazarus'* (Niemeyer), 1820; **D748**, *'Am Geburtstag des Kaisers'* (Deinhardstein), 1822; **D763**, *'Des Tages Weihe'* (unknown), 1822; **D815**, *'Gebet'* (Fouqué), 1824; **D826**, *'Der Tanz'* (?Schnitzer von Mecrau), 1828; **D875a**, *'Die Allmacht'* (Pyrker von Felsö-Eör), 1826; **D920**, *'Ständchen'* (Grillparzer), 1827

D930, *'Der Hochzietsbraten'* (Schober), 1828; **D936**, *'Kantate für Irene Kieswetter'* (anonymous Italian), 1827; **D942**, *'Mirjams Siegesang'* (Grillparzer), 1828; **D953**, *'Der 92

Psalm' (Hebrew text), 1828; **D954**, *'Glaube, Hoffnung und Liebe'* (Reil),

1828; **D985**, *'Gott in Ungewitter'* (Uz), ?1827

FOR MALE VOICES

D37, *'Die Advokaten'* (Engelhart), 1812; **D38**, *'Totengräberlied '* (Hölty), 1813; **D43**, *'Dreifach ist der Schritt der Zeit '* (1) (Schiller), 1813; **D51**, *'Unendliche Freude'* (Schiller), 1813; **D53**, *'Vorüber die stöhnende Klage'* (Schiller), 1813; **D54**, *'Unendliche Freude'* (2) (Schiller), 1813; **D55**, *'Selig durch die Liebe'* (Schiller), 1813; **D57**, *'Hier strecket der wallende Pilger'* (Schiller), 1813; **D58**, *'Dessen Fahne Donnerstürme wallte'* (Schiller), 1813; **D60**, *'Hier umarmen sich getreue Gatten'* (Schiller), 1813; **D62**, *'Thronend auf erhabnem Sitz'* (Schiller), 1813; **D63**, *'Wer die steile Sternenbahn'* (Schiller), 1813; **D64**, *'Majestäsche Sonnenrosse'* (Schiller), 1813; **D65**, *'Schmerz verzerret ihr Gesicht '* (Schiller), 1813; **D67**, *'Frisch atmet des Morgens lebendiger Hauch'* (Schiller), 1813

D70, *'Dreifach ist der Schritt der Zeit '* (Schiller), 1813; **D71**, *'Die zwei Tugendwege'* (Schiller), 1813; **D75**, *'Trinklied '* (*'Freunde, sammelt euch im Kreise'*) (Schäffer), 1813; **D80**, *'Zur Namensfeier meines Vaters'* (Schubert), 1813; **D88**, *'Verschunden sind die Schmerzen'* (Schubert), 1813

D110, *'Wer ist gross?'* (unknown), 1814; **D129**, *'Mailied '* (Hölty), 1815; **D132**, *'Lied beim Rundetanz'* (Salis-Seewis), 1815; **D133**, *'Lied im Freien'* (Salis-Seewis), 1815; **D140**, *'Klage um Ali Bey'* (1) (Claudius), 1815; **D147**, *'Bardengesang'* (Ossian), 1816; **D148**, *'Trinklied '* (*'Brüder! unser Erdenwallen'*) (Casteli), 1815; **D236**, *'Das Abendrot '* (Kosegarten), 1815; **D242**, *'Trinklied im Winter'* (Hölty), 1815; **D243**, *'Frühlingslied '* (*'Die

Luft ist blau'*) (Hölty), 1815; **D268**, *'Bergknappenlied '* (unknown), 1815; **D269**, *'Das Leben'* (Wannovius), 1815; **D277**, *'Punschlied '* (*'Vier Elemente innig gesellt '*) (Schiller), 1815

D330, *'Das Grab'* (2) (Salis-Seewis), 1815; **D331**, *'Der Entfernten'* (1) (Salis-Seewis), 1816; **D337**, *'Die Einsiedelei'* (Salis-Seewis), 1816; **D338**, *'An den Frühling'* (2) (Schiller), 1816; **D339**, *'Amors Macht '* (Matthisson), 1816; **D340**, *'Badelied '* (Matthisson), 1816; **D341**, *'Sylphen'* (Matthisson), 1816; D356, *'Trinklied '* (*'Funkeld im Becher'*) (unknown), 1816; **D364**, *'Fischerlied '* (2) (Salis-Seewis), 1816; **D377**, *'Das Grab'* (3) (Salis-Seewis), 1816; **D387**, *'Die Schlacht '* (2) (Schiller), 1816

D407, *'Beitrag zur Fünfzig jährigen Jubelfeier des Herrn Salieri'* (Schubert), 1816; **D422**, *'Naturgenuss'* (2) (Matthisson), 1816; **D423**, *'Andeken'* (Matthisson), 1816; **D424**, *'Erinnerungen'* (*'Am Seegestad '*) (Matthisson), 1816; **D425**, *'Lebensbild '* (unknown), 1816; **D426**, *'Trinklied '* (unknown), 1816; **D427**, *'Trinklied im Mai'* (Hölty), 1816; **D428**, *'Widerhall '* (*'Auf ewig dein'*) (Matthisson), 1816; **D441**, As D407, arranged for two tenors and bass, 1816; **D494**, *'Der Geistertanz'* (4) (Matthisson), 1816; **D513**, *'La pastorella al prato'* (Goldoni), 1817; **D538**, *'Gesang der Geister über den Wassern'* (Goethe), 1817; **D569**, *'Das Grab'* (Salis-Seewis), 1817; **D572**, *'Lied im freien'* (Salis-Seewis), 1817; **D598**, *'Das Dörfchen'* (unknown), 1817; **D635**, *'Leise, leise lasst uns singen'* (unknown), 1819; **D641**, *'Das Dörfchen'* (second version), 1819; **D656**, *'Sehnsucht '* (Goethe), 1819; **D657**, *'Ruhe, Schönstes Glück der Erde'* (unknown), 1819

D704, '*Gesang der Geister über den Wassern*' (Goethe), 1820; D705, '*Gesang des Geister über den Wassern*' (sketch) (Goethe), 1820; D709, '*Frühlingesang*' (Schober), before April 1822; D710, '*Im Gegenwärten Vergangenes*' (Goethe), 1821; D714, '*Gesang der Geister über den Wassern*' (Goethe), 1820; D724, '*Die nachtingall*' (Unger), 1821; D740, '*Frühlingsgesang*' (Schober), 1822; D747, '*Geist der Liebe*' (Matthisson), 1822; D778b, '*Ich hab in mich gesogen*' (Rückert), 1823

D809, '*Gondelfahrer*' (Mayrhofer), 1824; D822, '*Lied eines Kriegers*' (unknown), 1824; D825, '*Wehmut*' (Hüttenbrenner), 1826; D825a, '*Ewige Liebe*' (Schulze), 1826; D825b, '*Flucht*' (Lappe), 1825; D835, '*Bootgesang*' (Scott), 1825; D847, '*Trinklied aus dem 16 Jahrhundert*' (Gräffer), 1825; D848, '*Nachtmusik*' (Seckendorff),

1825; D865, '*Widerspruch*' (Seidl), 1826; D873a, '*Nachklänge*' (unknown), 1826; D875, '*Mondenschein*' (Schober), 1826; D892, '*Nachthelle*' (Seidl), 1826; D893, '*Grab und Mond*' (Seidl), 1826

D901, '*Wein und Liebe*' (Haug), 1827; D903, '*Zur guten Nacht*' (Rochlitz), 1827; D912, '*Schlachtlied*' (Klopstock), 1827; D913, '*Nachtgesang im Walde*' (Seidl), 1827; D914, '*Frühlingslied*' (Pollak), 1827; D916, '*Das stille Lied*' (Seegemund), 1827; D941, '*Hymnus an den Heiligen Geist*' (Schmidl), 1828; D948, '*Hymnus an den Heiligen Geist*' (other versions) (Schmidl), 1828; D964, '*Hymnus an den Heiligen Geist*' (other arrangement) (Schmidl), 1828; D983, '*Jünglingswonne*' (Matthisson), ?1822; D983a, '*Liebe*' (Schiller), ?1822; D983b, '*Zum Rundetanz*' (Salis-Seewis), ?1822; D983c, '*Die Nacht*' (?Krummacher), ?1822

FOR FEMALE OR UNSPECIFIED VOICES

D17, '*Quell' innocente figlio*', version 2 (Metastasio), 1812; D33, '*Entra l'uomo allor che nasce*' (Metastasio), 1812; D61, '*Ein jugendlicher Maienschwung*' (Schiller), 1813; D69, *Dreifach ist der Schritt der Zeit* (Schiller), 1813; D130, *Der Schnee zerrinnt* (1) (Hölty), 1815; D131, *Lacrimoso son io* (unknown), 1815; D169, *Trinklied vor der Schlacht* (Körner), 1815; D170, *Schwertlied* (Körner), 1815; D183, *Trinklied* ('*Ihr Freunde und du gold'ner Wein*') (Zettler), 1815; D189, *An die Freunde* (Schiller), 1815; D199, *Mailied* ('*Grüner wird die Au*') (Hölty), 1815

D202, *Mailied* ('*Der Schnee zerrinnt*') (Hölty), 1815; D203, *Der Morgenstern* (2) (Körner), 1815; D204, *Jägerlied* (Körner), 1815;

D205, *Lützows wilde Jagd* (Körner), 1815; D244, *Wilkommen, lieber schöner Mai* (Hölty), 1815; D253, *Punschlied: im Norden zu singen* (Schiller), 1815; D269, *Das Leben* (Wannovius), 1815

D357, *Gold'ner Schein, canon* (Mattthisson), 1816; D442, *Das grosse Halleluja* (Klopstock), 1816; D443, *Schlachtlied* (1) (Klopstock), 1816; D521, *Jagdlied* (Werner), 1817; D706, *Der 23 Psalm*, trans. (Mendelssohn), 1817; D757, *Gott in der Natur* (Kleist), 1822;

D836, *Coronach (Totengesang der Frauen und Mädchen)* (Scott), 1825; D873, *Canon, in A minor* (sketch) (unknown), 1826; D920, *Stänchen* (formerly D921) (Grillparzer), 1827; D988, *Liebe säuseln die Blätter*, Hölty, ?1815

RELIGIOUS WORKS

D24e, *Mass, in F* (fragment),
?1812; **D27**, *Salve Regina, in F*,
1812; **D31**, *Kyrie, in D minor*, 1812;
D45, *Kyrie, in B flat*, 1813; **D49**,
Kyrie, in D minor, 1813; **D56**, *Sanctus, in B flat*, 1813; **D66**, *Kyrie, in F*,
1813; **D71a**, *Alleluja, in F*, 1813;
D105, *Mass No.1, in F*, 1814; **D106**,
Salve Regina, in B flat, 1814; **D136**,
Offertory, in C, ?1815;
   D167, *Mass No.2, in G*, 1815;
D175, *Stabat mater, in G minor*,
1815; **D181**, *Offertory, in A minor*,
1815; **D184**, *Gradual: Benedictus,
Domine*, 1815; **D185**, *Dona nobis pacem, in F*, 1815; **D223**, *Salve regina,
in F*, 1815; **D324**, *Mass No.3, in B
flat*, 1815; **D379**, *Deutsches Salve regina, in F*, 1816; **D386**, *Salve regina,
in B flat*, 1816
   D452, *Mass No.4, in C*, 1816;

D453, *Requiem, in C minor*, 1816;
D460, *Tantum ergo, in C*, 1816;
D461, *Tantum ergo, in C*, 1816; **D486**,
Magnificat, in C, 1815; **D488**, *Auguste
iam coelestium, in G*, 1816; **D607**, *Evangelium Johannis* VI, in E, 1818; **D621**,
Deutsches Requiem, in G minor, 1818;
D676, *Salve regina, in A*, 1819;
D678, *Mass No.5, in A flat*, 1819;
D696, *Six antiphons for Palm Sunday*,
1820
   D730, *Tantum ergo, in B flat*, 1821;
D739, *Tantum ergo, in C*, 1814;
D750, *Tantum ergo, in D*, 1822; **D755**,
Kyrie, in A minor, 1822; **D811**, *Salve regina, in C*, 1824; **D872**, *Deutsche Messe*,
1827; **D950**, *Mass No.6, in E flat*,
1828; **D961**, *Benedictus, in A minor*
(alternative movement, D452),
1828; **D962**, *Tantum ergo, in E flat*,
1828; **D963**, *Offertory, in B flat*, 1828

THEATRICAL WORKS

D11, *Der Spiegelritter* (Kotzebue),
1811–12; **D84**, *Des Teufels Lustschloss*
(Kotzebue), 1813–15; **D137**, *Adrast* (Mayrhofer), 1817–19; **D190**,
Der vierjährige Posten (Körner),
1815; **D220**, *Fernando* (Stadler),
1815; **D239**, *Claudine von Villa Bella*
(Goethe), 1815; **D326**, *Die Freunde
von Salamanka* (Mayrhofer), 1815;
D435, *Die Bürgschaft* (unknown),
1816; **D644**, *Die Zauberharfe* (Hofmann), 1820; **D647**, *Die Zwill-*

ingsbrüder (Hofmann), 1819; **D701**,
Sakuntala (Neumann), 1820; **D723**,
Duet and aria for Hérold's Das Zauberglöckchen (Théaulon), 1821; **D732**, *Alfonso und Estrella* (Schober), 1821–22;
D787, *Die Verschworenen* (Castelli),
1823; **D791**, *Rüdiger* (?Mosel), 1823;
D796, *Fierabras* (Kupelweiser),
1823; **D797**, *Rosamunde, Fürsten von
Zypern* (Chézy), 1823; **D918**, *Der
Graf von Gleichen* (Bauernfeld), 1827;
D981, *Der Minnesänger* (lost), 1827

SONATAS, FANTASIAS AND SHORTER WORKS FOR PIANO

D2e, *Fantasie, in C minor*, 1822;
D13, *Fugue, in D minor*, 1812; **D14**,
Overture (lost sketch), 1812; **D21**,
Six Variations, in F (lost sketch),
1812; **D24a**, *Fugue, in C*, 1812;
D24b, *Fugue, in G*, 1812; **D24c**,
Fugue, in D minor, 1812; **D24d**,
Fugue, in C (fragment), 1812; **D29**,
Andante, in C, 1812; **D37a**, *Fugal
sketches, in B flat*, 1813; **D41a**, *Fugue*,

in E minor (fragment), 1813; **D71b**,
Fugue, in E minor (fragment), 1813;
D154, *Allegro, in E* (sketch of D157),
1815; **D156**, *Ten Variations, in F*, 1815;
D157, *Sonata, in E* (unfinished),
1815; **D178**, *Adagio, in G*, 1815;
D279, *Sonata, in C*, 1815
   D346, *Allegretto, in C* (fragment),
1816; **D347**, *Allegretto moderato, in C*
(fragment), 1813; **D348**, *Andantino,*

in C (fragment), 1816; **D349**, *Adagio, in C* (fragment), 1816; **D459**, *Sonata, in E* (fragment), 1816; **D459a**, *Fünf Klavierstücke Nos.3–5*, 1816; **D505**, *Adagio, in D flat* (original slow movement of D625), 1816?; **D506**, *Rondo, in E* (finale for D566?), 1817; **D537**, *Sonata, in A minor*, 1817; **D557**, *Sonata, in A flat*, 1817; **D566**, *Sonata, in E minor*, 1817; **D567**, *Sonata, in D flat* (first version of D568), 1817; **D568**, *Sonata, in E flat*, 1817; **D570**, *Scherzo, in D*, 1817; **D571**, *Sonata, in F sharp minor* (unfinished), 1817; **D575**, *Sonata, in B*, 1817; **D576**, *Thirteen Variations on a Theme by Hüttenbrenner*, 1817; **D593**, *Two Scherzi (B flat, D flat)*, 1817

D604, *Andante, in A*, 1817; **D605**, *Fantasia, in C* (unfinished), 1821–23; **D605a**, *Fantasy, in C* : 'Grazer Fantasie', 1818; **D606**, *March, in E*, 1818; **D612**, *Adagio, in E*, 1818; **D613**, *Sonata, in C* (unfinished), 1818; **D625**, *Sonata, in F minor* (unfinished), 1818; **D655**,

Sonata, in C sharp minor (fragment), 1819; **D664**, *Sonata, in A*, 1819 or 1825; **D718**, *Variations on a Waltz by Diabelli, in C minor*, 1821; **D749a**, *Overture to 'Alfonso und Estrella'*, 1822; **D760**, *Fantasy in C* : 'Wandererfantasie', 1822; **D769a**, *Sonata, in E minor* (fragment), 1823; **D780**, *Six Moments Musicaux*, 1823–28; **D784**, *Sonata, in A minor*, 1823

D817, *Ungarische Melodie, in B minor*, 1824; **D840**, *Sonata, in C* : 'Reliquie' (unfinished), 1825; **D850**, *Sonata, in D*, 1825; **D894**, *Sonata, in G* ('Fantasie'), 1826; **D899**, *Four Impromptus: in C minor, E flat, G flat, A flat*, 1827; **D900**, *Allegretto, in C minor* (fragment), after 1820; **D915**, *Allegretto, in C minor*, 1827; **D916b**, *Piano piece, in C* (sketch), 1827; **D916c**, *Piano piece, in C minor* (sketch), 1827; **D935**, *Four Impromptus: in F minor, A flat, B flat, F minor*, 1827; **D946**, *Drei Klavierstücke: in E flat minor, E flat, C*, 1828; **D958**, *Sonata, in C minor*, 1828; **D959**, *Sonata, in A*, 1828; **D960**, *Sonata, in B flat*, 1828

DANCES FOR PIANO

D19b, *Waltzes and march* (lost), 1812 or 1813; **D22**, *Twelve minuets with trios* (lost), 1812; **D41**, *Thirty minuets with trios* (10 lost), 1813; **D91**, *Two minuets (in D, A) and trios*, 1813; **D128**, *Twelve Wiener Deutsche*, 1812; **D135**, *Deutscher, in E, with trio*, 1815; **D139**, *Deutscher, in C sharp, with trio*, 1815; **D145**, *12 Waltzes*, 1815–21; **D146**, *20 Waltzes (Letzte Walzer)*, 1815, 1823

D158, *Ecossaise, in D minor, F*, 1815; **D277a**, *Minuet, in A minor*, 1815; **D299**, *Twelve Ecossaises*, 1815; **D334**, *Minuet, in A, with trio*, 1815; **D335**, *Minuet, in E, with 2 trios*, 1813; **D365**, *36 Originaltänze (Erste Walzer)*, 1816–21; **D366**, *17 Ländler*, 1816–24; **D378**, *Eight Ländler, in B flat*, 1816; **D380**, *Three*

Minuets, with trios, 1816; **D420**, *Twelve Deutsche*, 1816; **D421**, *Six Ecossaises, in E flat*, 1816; **D511**, *Ecossaise, in E flat*, 1817; **D529**, *Eight Ecossaises*, 1817

D600, *Minuet, in C sharp minor*, 1814; **D610**, *Trio, in E*, 1818; **D640**, *Two Dances* (date unknown); **D643**, *Deutscher, in C sharp minor, and Ecossaise, in E flat*, 1819; **D680**, *Two Ländler* (date unknown); **D681**, *Two Ländler* (date unknown); **D697**, *Six Ecossaises, in A flat*, 1820; **D722**, *Deutscher, in G flat*, 1821; **D734**, *16 Ländler and 2 Ecossaises (Wiener-Damen Ländler)*, 1822; **D735**, *Galop and eight Ecossaises*, 1822; **D769**, *Two Deutsche*, 1823–24; **D779**, *34 Valses Sentimentales*, 1823; **D781**, *Twelve Ecossaises*, 1823; **D782**, *Ecossaise, in D*, 1823;

D783, *16 Deutsche and 2 Ecossaises*, 1823–24; D790, *Twelve Deutsche (Ländler)*, 1823–24

D816, *Three Ecossaises*, 1824; D820, *Six Deutsche*, 1824; D841, *Two Deutsche (in F, G)*, 1825; D844, *Waltz, in G (Albumblatt)*, 1825; D924, *Twelve Grazer Walzer*, 1827; D925, *Grazer Galopp, in C*, 1827; D969, *Twelve Walzes (Valses Nobles)*, 1826; D970, *Six Ländler* (date unknown); D971, *Three Deutsche (in A minor, A, E)*, 1822; D972, *Three Deutsche (in D flat, A flat, A)* (date unknown); D973, *Three Deutsche (in E, E, A flat)* (date unknown); D974, *Two Deutsche, in D flat* (date unknown); D975, *Deutscher, in D* (date unknown); D976, *Cotillon, in E flat*, 1825; D977, *Eight Ecossaises* (date unknown); D978, *Waltz, in A flat*, 1825; D979, *Waltz, in G*, 1826; D980, *Two Waltzes: in G , B minor*, 1826; D980d, *Waltz, in C*, 1827

PIANO WORKS FOR FOUR HANDS

D1, *Fantasie, in G*, 1810; D1b, *Fantasie, in G* (fragment), 1810 or 1811; D1c, *Sonata, in F* (fragment), 1810 or 1811; D9, *Fantasie, in G minor*, 1813; D48, *Fantasie, in C minor*, 1813; D592, *Overture, in D 'im Italienische Stile'* (arrangement of D590), 1817; D597, *Overture, in C 'im Italienische Stile'* (arrangement of D591), 1817; D599, *Four Polonaises*, 1818; D602, *Three Marches Héroïques (B minor, C, D)*, 1818 or 1824; D603, *Introduction and Four Variations on an Original Theme*, 1824; D608, *Rondo, in D ('Notre amitié est invariable')*, 1824; D617, *Sonata, in B flat*, 1818; D618, *Deutscher, in G*, 1818; D618a, *Polonaise and Trio* (sketch), 1818; D624, *Eight Variations on a French Song*, 1818; D668, *Overture, in G minor*, 1819; D675, *Overture, in F*, 1819

D733, *Three Marches Militaires (in D, G, E flat)*, 1818; D773, *Overture to 'Alfonso und Estrella'*, 1823; D798, *Overture to 'Fierabras'*, 1823; D812, *Sonata in D : 'Grand Duo'*, 1824; D818, *Divertissement à l'hongroise, in G minor*, 1824; D823, *Six Grandes Marches*, 1824; D824, *Six Polonaises*, 1826; D859, *Grande Marche Funèbre, in C minor*, 1825; D885, *Grande Marche Héroïque, in A minor*, 1826; D886, *Two Marches Caractéristiques, in C*, 1826

D908, *Eight Variations on a Theme from Hérold's 'Marie', in C*, 1827; D928, *March, in G : 'Kindermarsch'*, 1827; D940, *Fantasie, in F minor*, 1828; D947, *Allegro, in A minor : 'Lebensstürme'*, 1828; D951, *Rondo, in A*, 1828; D952, *Fugue, in F minor*, 1828; D968, *Allegro Moderato, in C and Andante (Sonatine)*, 1818

CHAMBER WORKS

D2c, *String Quartet, in F* (fragment), ?1811; D2d, *Six Minuets*, 1811; D2f, *Trio of a minuet, in C*, 1811; D3, *String Quartet, in C* (fragment), 1812; D8, *Overture, in C minor*, 1811; D8a, *Arrangement of D8*, 1811; D18, *String Quartet, in B flat*, 1810 or 1811; D19, *String Quartet* (lost), 1810 or 1811; D19a, *String Quartet* (lost), 1810 or 1811; D20, *Overture, in B flat* (lost), 1812; D28, *Trio (sonata in one movement) in B flat*, 1812; D32, *String Quartet, in C*, 1812; D36, *String Quartet, in B flat*, 1813; D46, *String Quartet, in C*, 1813; D68, *String Quartet, in B flat* (fragment), 1813; D72, *Wind Octet, in F*, 1813; D72a, *Allegro, in F* (fragment), 1813; D74, *String Quartet, in D*, 1813; D79, *Wind Nonet, in E flat minor*, 1813;

D86, *Minuet, in D*, 1813; D87, *String Quartet, in E flat*, 1813; D89, *Five minuets and trios*, 1813; D90, *Five Deutsches and trios*, 1813; D94, *String Quartet, in D*, 1811 or 12; D94b, *Five minuets and Deutsche* (lost), 1813; D96, *Trio, in G*, 1814

D103, *String Quartet, in C minor* (fragment), 1814; D111a, *String Trio, in B flat*, 1814; D173, *String Quartet, in G minor*, 1815; D353, *String Quartet, in E*, 1816; D354, *Four Komische Ländler, in D*, 1816; D355, *Eight Ländler, in F sharp minor*, 1816; D370, *Nine Ländler, in D*, 1816; D374, *Eleven Ländler, in B flat*, 1816; D384, *Sonata, in D, violin and piano*, 1816; D385, *Sonata, in A minor, violin and piano*, 1816; D408, *Sonata, in G minor, violin and piano*, 1816; D471, *String Trio, in B flat* (fragment), 1816; D487, *Adagio*

and Rondo Concertante, in F, 1816

D574, *Sonata, in A, violin and piano*, 1817; D581, *String Trio, in B flat*, 1817; D597a, *Variations, in A, for solo violin* (lost), 1817; D601, *Overture for string quartet* (fragment), in B flat, 1816; D667, *Piano Quintet, in A* : 'Die Forelle', 1819; D703, *String Quartet movement, in C minor* : 'Quartettsatz', 1820; D802, *Introduction and Variations for flute and piano*, 1824; D803, *Octet, in F*, 1824; D804, *String Quartet, in A minor*, 1824; D810, *String Quartet, in D minor* : 'Der Tod und das Mädchen', 1824; D821, *Sonata in A minor* : 'Arpeggione', 1824; D887, *String Quartet, in G*, 1826; D895, *Rondo Brillant in B minor for violin and piano*, 1826; D898, *Piano Trio in B flat*, 1827; D929, *Piano Trio in E flat*, 1827; D934, *Fantasy in C for violin and piano*, 1827; D956, *String Quintet in C*, 1828

ORCHESTRAL WORKS

D2a, *Overture, in D* (fragment: formerly D996), ?1811; D2b, *Symphony, in D* (fragment), ?1811; D4, *Overture, in D for Albrecht's comedy 'Der Teufel als Hydraulicus'*, ?1812; D12, *Overture, in D*, 1811 or 1812; D26, *Overture, in D*, 1812; D39a, *Three minuets and trios* (lost), 1813; D71c, *Orchestral fragment, in D*, 1813; D82, *Symphony No.1, in D*, 1813; D94a, *Orchestral fragment, in B flat*, 1814

D125, *Symphony No.2, in B flat*, 1814–15; D200, *Symphony No.3, in D*, 1815; D345, *Concertstück in D, for violin and orchestra*, 1816; D417, *Symphony No.4 in C minor* : 'Tragic', 1816; D438, *Rondo in A, for violin and orchestra*, 1816; D470, *Overture, in B flat*, 1816; D485, *Symphony No.5, in B flat*, 1816

D556, *Overture, in D*, 1817; D580, *Polonaise in B flat for violin and orchestra*, 1817; D589, *Symphony No.6, in C*, 1817–18; D590, *Overture, in D, 'in the Italian style'* (as duet D592), 1817; D591, *Overture, in C, 'in the Italian style'* (as duet D597), 1817

D615, *Symphony, in D* (sketches for 2 movements), 1818; D648, *Overture, in E minor* (possibly for 'Adrast'), 1819; D708a, *Symphony, in D* (sketches), after 1820; D729, *Symphony No.7, in E* (sketched in score), 1821; D759, *Symphony No.8, in B minor* : 'Unfinished', 1822; D849, *'Gmunden-Gastein' Symphony* (probably identical with D944), 1825; D936a, *Symphony No.10, in D* (sketches), mid-1828; D944, *Symphony No.9, in C* : 'The Great', 1825–?1828

RECOMMENDED RECORDINGS

These recordings are commercially available at the time of writing. Works are listed first, followed by details of the recording, artists and disc number. All serial numbers given apply to compact disc, but some recordings can also be bought on conventional tape cassette. Inevitably, to buy every CD here would create a large degree of duplication. There's much to be said for not limiting your outlook to one sacred version, of course; but listeners can rest assured that any of the recordings mentioned below will give pleasure from beginning to end.

A list of abbreviations used in the following pages appears at the end of this section.

SONGS

Lieder, 1811–1828
◇ Fischer-Dieskau (bar) / Moore ⊗ DG 437 214-2GX21 (three volumes: 21 discs)

Cycles: *Die schöne Müllerin; Winterreise; Schwanengesang*
◇ Fischer-Dieskau (bar) / Moore ⊗ DG 720 059 (3-disc set)

Die schöne Müllerin (D795)
◇ Bostridge (ten), Fischer-Dieskau (reader) / Johnson ⊗ Hyperion CDJ33025
◇ Also recommended: Schreier (ten) / Schiff ⊗ Decca 430 414-2DH

Winterreise (D911)
◇ Schreier (ten) / Schiff ⊗ Decca 436 122-2DH
◇ Consider too: Fischer-Dieskau / Brendel ⊗ Philips 411 463-2PH

Schwanengesang (D957)
◇ Schreier (ten) / Schiff ⊗ Decca 425 612-2
◇ Consider too: Fassbaender (mezzo) / Reimann ⊗ DG 429766-2

Lieder recital: *'An die Musik'* (D547); *'Im Frühling'* (D882);

'Wehmut' (D772); *'Ganymed'* (D544); *'Das Lied im Grünen'* (D917); *'Gretchen am Spinnrade'* (D118); *'Nähe des Geliebten'* (D162); *'Die junge Nonne'* (D828); *'An Sylvia'* (D891); *'Auf dem Wasser du singen'* (D774); *'Nachtviolen'* (D752); *'Der Musensohn'* (D764)
◇ Schwarzkopf (sop) / Fischer ⊗ EMI mono CDH7 64026-2

Elizabeth Schumann sings selected Schubert Lieder: *'An die Nachtigall'* (D497); *'Die Forelle'* (D550); *'Ave Maria'* (D839); *'An die Musik'* (D547); *'Auf dem Wasser zu singen'* (D774); *'Des Fischers Liebesglück'* (D933); *'Der Musensohn'* (D764); *'Fischerweise'* (D881); *'Gretchen am Spinnrade'* (D118); *'Liebesbotschaft'* (D951 No.1); *'Nacht und Träume'* (D827); *'Seligkeit'* (D433); *'Nähe des Geliebten'* (D162); *'Lachen und Weinen'* (D777); *'Frühlingstraum'* (D911 No.11); *'Der Einsame'* (D800); *'Nachtviolen'* (D752); *'An die Geliebte'* (D303); *'Wiegenlied'* (D498); *'Der Schmetterling'* (D633); *'Des Baches Wiegenlied'* (D795 No.25); *'Der Jüngling und der Tod'* (D545); *'Das Heimweh'* (D456);

'*Dass sie hier gewesen*' (D775); '*Der Vollmond Strahlt*' (D797); '*Die Junge Nonne*' (D828)

◊ Schumann (sop) / various accompanists
⊗ Minerva (Kingdom) mono MN A22

Lieder recital, 'An die Musik': '*Gruppe aus dem Tartarus*' (D583); '*Litanei auf dem Fest Allerseelen*' (D343); '*An die Leier*' (D737); '*Lachen und Weinen*' (D777); '*Schwanengesang*' (D957): '*Ständchen*', '*Das Fischermädchen*', '*Die Taubenpost*'; '*Meeres Stille*' (D216); '*Der Wanderer*' (D489); '*Erlkönig*' (D328); '*Der Tod und das Mädchen*' (D531); '*Heidenröslein*' (D257); '*Wanderers Nachtlied 2*' (D768); '*An die Musik*' (D547); '*Auf der Bruck*' (D853); '*Schäfers Klagelied*' (D121); '*An Sylvia*' (D891); '*Du bist die Ruh*' (D776); '*An die Laute*' (D905); '*Rastlose Liebe*' (D138); '*Ganymed*' (D544); '*Der Musensohn*' (D764)

◊ Terfel (bass-bar) / Martineau
⊗ DG 445 294-2GH

Goethe Lieder: '*Am Flusse*' (D160); '*Trost in Tränen*' (D120); '*Schäfers Klagelied*' (D121); '*Meeres Stille*' (D216); '*Heidenröslein*' (D257); '*Jägers Abendlied*' (D368); '*Sehnsucht*' (D123); '*Die Liebe*' (D210); '*Rastlose Liebe*' (D138); '*Nähe des Geliebten*' (D162); '*Der Fis-*cher*' (D225); '*Erster Verlust*' (D226); '*Der König von Thule*' (D367); '*Wer sich der Einsamkeit ergibt*' (D478); '*Wer nie sein Brot mit Tränen ass*' (D479); '*An die Türen will ich schleichen*' (D480); '*An Schwager Kronos*' (D369); '*An Mignon*' (D161); '*Ganymed*' (D544); '*An die Entfernte*' (D765); '*Versunken*' (D715); '*An den Mond*' (D259); '*Der Musensohn*' (D764); '*Auf dem See*' (D543); '*Geistes Gruss*' (D142)

◊ Prégardien (ten) / Staier (fp)
⊗ Deutsche Harmonia Mundi 05472 77342-2

Lieder recital: '*Ave Maria*' ('*Ellens Gesang 3*') (D839); '*Ganymed*' (D544); '*Kennst du das Land*' (D321); '*Heiss mich nicht reden*' (D877 No.2); '*So lasst mich scheinen*' (D877 No.3); '*Nur wer die Sehnsucht kennt*' (D877 No.4); '*Liebhaber in allen Gestalten*' (D558); '*Heidenröslein*' (D257); '*Nähe des Geliebten*' (D162); '*Die Forelle*' (D550); '*Auf dem Wasser zu singen*' (D774); '*Im Abendrot*' (D799); '*Ständchen*' (D889); '*Du bist die Ruh*' (D776); '*Gretchen am Spinnrade*' (D118); '*Gretchens Bitte*' (D564); '*Der Hirt auf dem Felsen*' (D965)*.

◊ Bonney (sop) / Parsons (pf) / *Kam (clarinet)
⊗ Teldec 4509-90873-2

From the Hyperion Schubert Edition

Volume 1: '*Der Jungling am Bache*' (D30); '*Thekla*' (D73); '*Schäfers Klagelied*' (D121); '*Nähe des Geliebten*' (D162); '*Meeres Stille*' (D216); '*Amalia*' (D195); '*Die Erwartung*' (D159); '*Wanderers Nachtlied* (1)' (D224); '*Der Fischer*' (D225); '*Erster Verlust*' (D226); '*Wonne der Wehmut*' (D260); '*An den Mond*' (D296); '*Das Geheimnis*' (D250); '*Lied*' (D284); '*Der Flüchtling*' (D402); '*Anden Frühling*' (D402); '*Der Alpenjäger*' (D588); '*Der Pilgrim*' (D794); '*Sehnsucht*' (D636)

◊ Baker (mezzo) / Johnson
⊗ CDJ33001

Volume 21: '*Schlaflied*' (D527); '*Sehnsucht*' (D516); '*Liebe*' (D522); '*Die Forelle*' (D550); '*Nur wer die Liebe kennt*' (D513a); '*Flug der Zeit*' (D515); '*Trost*' (D523); '*Die Abgeblühte Linde*' (D514); '*Das Lied vom Reifen*' (D532); '*An eine Quelle*' (D530); '*An die Musik*' (D547);

'Der Schäfer und der Reiter' (D517);
'Hänflings Liebeswerbung' (D552);
'Schweizerlied' (D559); 'Liebhafer in
allen Gestalten' (D558); 'Abschied'
(D578); 'Erlafsee' (D586); 'Lied
eines Kindes' (D596); 'Evangelium Jo-
hannis' (D607); 'Lob der Tränen'
(D711); 'Grablied für die Mutter'
(D616); 'Der Blumenbrief' (D622);
'Blondel zu Marien' (D626); 'Vom
Mitleiden Mariä' (D632)
◊ Edith Mathis (sop) / Johnson
⊗ CDJ33021.
**Volume 18, 'Schubert and
the Strophic Song':** including 'Im
Frühling' (D882), 'Über Wildemann'
(D884) & 'Auf der Bruck' (D853)
◊ Schreier (ten) / Johnson
⊗ CDJ 33018
**Volume 8, 'Schubert and the
Nocturne':** including 'Erlkönig'
(D328), 'Ständchen' (D920)
◊ Walker (sop) / Johnson

⊗ CDJ 33008
**Volume 11, 'Schubert and
Death':** including 'Der Tod und das
Mädchen' (D531)
◊ Fassbaender (mezzo) /
Johnson ⊗ CDJ 33011
**Volume 14, 'Schubert and
Classical Antiquity':** including
'Gruppe aus dem Tartarus' (D396,
D583); 'Die Götter Griechenlands'
(D677)
◊ Hampson (bar) / Johnson
⊗ CDJ33014
**Volume 16, 'Schubert and
Schiller':** including 'An die Freude'
(D189)
◊ Allen (bar) / Johnson
⊗ CDJ 33016
**Volume 23, 'The Songs of
1816':** including Gesänge des
Harfners aus 'Wilhelm Meister' (D478)
◊ Prégardien (ten) / Johnson
⊗ CDJ 33023

Consider too:

Lieder Recital
◊ Lott (sop) / Johnson
⊗ IMP PCD2016
'Schubert in Full Flower', in-
cluding: 'Suleika 1 & 2'

◊ Lott (sop) / Johnson
⊗ Hyperion CDJ33019
Lieder Recital
◊ Keenlyside (bar) / Martineau
⊗ EMI CD-EMX2224

MUSIC FOR PIANO

Complete Piano Sonatas
◊ Kempff ⊗ DG 423 496-2GX7
(7-disc set); digital
recommendation (available
November 1996): Schiff, Decca
448 390-2
Duets: Overture in F (D675); Vari-
ations from Hérold's 'Marie' (D908);
Rondo in D (D608); Marches
Héroïques (D602); Fantasie in F minor
(D940); Variations in B flat (D603,
968a); Divertissement à la hongroise
(D818); six Polonaises (D824)
◊ Tal and Groethuysen
⊗ Sony S2K5895 (2-disc set)
Sonata No.8 in E flat (D568)

[with Sonata in C Minor (D958)]
◊ Schiff ⊗ Decca 440 308-2
Sonatas: No.9 in B (D575); No.11
in F minor (D625) [with Moments
Musicaux (D780) Nos.1, 3 & 6]
◊ Richter ⊗ Olympia OCD 286
Sonatas: No.9 in B (D575); No.15
in C (D840); No.18 in G (D894)
◊ Richter ⊗ Philips 438 483-PH2
(2-disc set)
**Piano Sonata No.13 in A
(D664)** [with Sonata in B flat
(D960)]
◊ Lupu ⊗ Decca 440 295-2
Wanderer Fantasy (D760) [with
Dvořák's Piano Concerto]

◊ Richter ⊗ EMI CDC7 47967-2
[with Schubert's D845 *Sonata*]
◊ Pollini ⊗ DG 419 672-2
Sonatas: *No.14 in A minor* (D784);
No.17 in D (D850)
◊ Brendel
⊗ Philips 422-063-2PH
Sonatas: *No.16 in A minor* (D845);
No.18 in G (D894)
◊ Lupu ⊗ Decca 417 640-2DH
Sonata in No.17 in D (D850)
[with D959 & D960 *sonatas*;
Moments Musicaux (D780) Nos.1–6;
March in E (D606)]
◊ Schnabel ⊗ EMI CHS764259-2
(2-disc set – historic mono
performance)
Sonata No.17 in D (D850);
Moments Musicaux (D780)
Nos.1-6 [with *Impromptus Nos.3
& 4* (D899)]
◊ Curzon ⊗ Decca 443 570-2
Impromptus: *Nos.1–4* (D899);
Nos.1–4 (D935)
◊ Perahia ⊗ Sony CK 37291
◊ Lupu ⊗ Decca 411711-2DH

Fantasia in F minor for Four
Hands (D940) [with Mozart's *So-
nata for Two Pianos* (K448)]
◊ Perahia, Lupu
⊗ Sony SK39551
Sonata No.19 in C minor
(D958); Moments Musicaux
(D780) Nos.1–6
◊ Lupu ⊗ Decca 417 785-2
Sonatas: *No.19 in C minor* (D958);
No.20 in A (D959)
◊ Pollini ⊗ DG 427 327-2
Sonata No.21 in B flat (D960)
[with concert of *Impromptus* and
Moments Musicaux]
◊ Kempff
⊗ DG Classikon 439 462-2
Digital recommendation:
◊ Lupu [with *Sonata in A*
(D664)]
⊗ Decca 440 295-2
Also commended:
◊ Kovacevich [with 12 *German
Dances* (D790); *Allegretto in C
minor* (D915)]
⊗ EMI CDC5 55359-2

CHAMBER MUSIC

String Quartet in A flat (D87);
String Trios in B flat (D471,
D581)
◊ L'Archibudelli
⊗ Sony Vivarte SK 53982
Violin Sonata in A major
(D574); Rondo Brillant in B
minor (D895); Fantasy in C
major (D934)
◊ Kremer / Afanassiev
⊗ DG 431 654-2GH
'Trout' Quintet (D667) [with
String Quartet No.14 in D minor
(D810)]
◊ Curzon / Vienna Octet
⊗ Decca 417 459-2DM
◊ Digital recommendation:
Schiff / Hagen Quartet
⊗ Decca 411 975-2DH
Piano Trios: *in B* (D28); *B flat*
(D898); *E flat* (D929) [with *Not-

turno* (D897) & *String Trios* (D471,
D581)]
◊ Beaux Arts Trio / Grumiaux
Trio
⊗ Philips 438 700-2PM2 (double
disc)
Octet in F major (D803)
◊ Hausmusik (on period
instruments)
⊗ EMI CDC7 54118-2
◊ Consider too (budget price):
Vienna Octet [with *Minuet*
and *Finale* of D72]
⊗ Decca 430-516-2DH
Also commended:
◊ Gaudier Ensemble
⊗ ASV CDDCA694
Late String Quartets and Quar-
tet fragments: D703, D804, D810
& D887
◊ With *Quintet* (D956) and

Quartet (D112): Lindsay Quartet ⊗ ASV CD DCS 417 (4-CD set)

♦ Without D956 *Quintet*: Melos Quartet ⊗ HMC90 1408-9 (2-CD set)

String Quartet No.13 in A minor (D804) [with *Quartet in B flat* (D112)]

♦ Lindsay Quartet
⊗ ASV CD DA 593

String Quartet No.14 in D minor (D810) [with '*Trout*' *Quintet* (D667)]

♦ Vienna Philharmonic Quartet
⊗ Decca 417 459-2DM

♦ Among digital versions, consider [with an adequate '*Trout*' *Quintet*]: Vermeer Quartet ⊗ Teldec 9301 74783-2; or [with '*Quartettsatz*' (D703)]: Lindsay Quartet
⊗ ASV CD DCA 560

String Quartets: *No.14 in D minor* (D810); *No.15 in G* (D887)

♦ Busch Quartet

⊗ EMI Références mono CDH7 69795-2

Sonata in A minor (D812): 'Arpeggione' [with Debussy and Schumann]

♦ Rostropovich / Britten
⊗ Decca 417 833-2DH

String Quartet No.15 in G (D887)

♦ Lindsay Quartet
⊗ ASV CD DCA 661

String Quintet in C (D956)

♦ (With Schoenberg's *Verklärte Nacht*) Hollywood Quartet / Reher, Testament
⊗ mono SBT 1031

♦ Mid-price (with Schubert's *Symphony No.5*, conducted by Casals): Stern, Schneider, Katims, Casals, Tortelier
⊗ Sony mono SMK 58992

Digital recommendation:

♦ Alban Berg Quartet / Schiff
⊗ EMI CDC7 47018-2

♦ Also commended: Lindsay Quartet / Cummings
⊗ ASV CD DCA 537

SYMPHONIES

Complete Symphonies: *Nos.1–6; 8–9*

♦ Harnoncourt, Concertgebouw
⊗ Teldec 4509 91184-2 (4-disc set)

♦ Abbado, COE ⊗ DG 423 653-2GH (5-disc set with *Rosamunde* music and Joachim's orchestration of the *Grand Duo*, D812)

Symphonies: *No.3 in D* (D200); *No.5 in B flat* (D485); *No.6 in C* (D589)

♦ Beecham, RPO
⊗ EMI CDCM7 69750-2

Symphonies: *Nos.3 in D* (D200); *4 in C minor: 'Tragic'* (D417)

♦ Abbado, COE
⊗ DG 423 653-2GH

Symphonies: *No.5 in B flat* (D485); *No.6 in C* (D589)

♦ Abbado, COE ⊗ DG 423 654-2GH

Symphony No.8 in B minor (D759)

♦ A subtle and safe (some might say, too safe) first choice is Harnoncourt and the Concertgebouw (with *Symphonies 3 & 5*)
⊗ Teldec 4509 97512-2

♦ More controversially, but as valuable adjuncts to received opinion: Kleiber, VPO (with a fast account of the D200 *Symphony*) ⊗ DG 415 601-2

♦ Sinopoli, Philharmonia (with Mendelssohn's '*Italian*' *Symphony*) ⊗ DG 445 514-2

◇ Also recommended: Abbado, COE (with *Rosamunde* excerpts) ⊗ DG 437 019-2 (with *Symphony No.9* : double disc, in effect mid-price)

◇ Wand, BPO
⊗ RCA 09026 68314-2

Symphony No.9 in C (D944)

◇ Harnoncourt, Concertgebouw
⊗ Teldec 4509 97512-2

◇ Also recommended: (With *Rosamunde Overture*) Abbado, COE ⊗ DG 423 656-2

◇ mid-price: Solti, VPO
⊗ Decca 430 747-2DM

◇ on period instruments: Mackerras, OAE ⊗ Virgin Classics VC7 58669-2

OPERA, CHORAL AND STAGE MUSIC

Mass No.5 in A flat (D678); Deutsche Messe (D872)

◇ Weil: Vienna Boys' Choir, Chorus Viennensis, OAE (period performance)
⊗ Sony Vivarte SK53984

Alfonso und Estrella (D732)

◇ Suitner: Berlin Radio Chorus, Berlin Staatskapelle
⊗ Berlin Classics BC2156-2

Fierabras (D796)

◇ Abbado: Arnold Schoenberg Choir, COE
⊗ DG 427 341-2

Incidental music to Rosamunde (D797) (complete)

◇ Abbado: Otter (sop), Ernst Senff Choir, COE
⊗ DG 431 655-2GH

Masses 1–6 and shorter choral works

◇ Sawallisch: Bavarian Radio Chorus, Bavarian RSO
⊗ EMI Sawallisch Edition CMS7 64778-2 and CMS7 64783-2 (4- and 3-disc sets)

◆

Abbreviations

ASV	Academy Sound and Vision	**mezzo**	mezzo-soprano
BPO	Berlin Philharmonic Orchestra	**OAE**	Orchestra of the Age of Enlightenement
bar	baritone	**pf**	pianoforte (present-day piano)
COE	Chamber Orchestra of Europe	**RSO**	Radio Symphony Orchestra
DG	Deutsche Grammophon	**sop**	soprano
fp	fortepiano	**ten**	tenor
HM	Harmonia Mundi	**VPO**	Vienna Philharmonic Orchestra

Index

CLASSIC *f*M
LIFELINES

With 4.8 million listeners every week, *Classic fM* is now the most listened-to national commercial radio station in the UK. With the launch of *Classic fM Lifelines*, Pavilion Books and *Classic fM* are creating an affordable series of elegantly designed short biographies that will put everyone's favourite composers into focus.

Written with enthusiasm and in a highly accessible style, the *Classic fM Lifelines* series will become the Everyman of musical biographies. Titles for the series have been chosen from *Classic fM*'s own listener surveys of the most popular composers.

TITLES PUBLISHED:

Johannes Brahms
Jonathon Brown
ISBN: 1 85793 967 0

Claude Debussy
Jonathon Brown
ISBN: 1 85793 972 7

Edward Elgar
David Nice
ISBN: 1 85793 977 8

Gustav Mahler
Julian Haylock
ISBN: 1 85793 982 4

Sergei Rachmaninov
Julian Haylock
ISBN: 1 85793 944 1

Franz Schubert
Stephen Jackson
ISBN: 1 85793 987 5

£4.99 each book

FORTHCOMING TITLES:

- J.S. Bach
- Ludwig van Beethoven
- Benjamin Britten

- Joseph Haydn
- Dmitri Shostakovich
- Ralph Vaughan Williams

CLASSIC *f*M LIFELINES

To purchase any of the books in the *Classic fM Lifelines* series
simply fill in the order form below and post or fax it,
together with your remittance, to the address below.

Please send the titles ticked below
(*published spring 1997)

Johannes Brahms	☐	*J.S. Bach	☐
Claude Debussy	☐	*Ludwig van Beethoven	☐
Edward Elgar	☐	*Benjamin Britten	☐
Gustav Mahler	☐	*Joseph Haydn	☐
Sergei Rachmaninov	☐	*Dmitri Shostakovich	☐
Franz Schubert	☐	*Ralph Vaughan Williams	☐

Number of titles @ £4.99 _____   Value: £_____

Add 10% of total value for postage and packing   Value: £_____

Total value of order: £_____

I enclose a cheque (UK only) payable to Pavilion Books Ltd ☐

OR

Please charge my credit card account ☐

I wish to pay by: Visa ☐ MasterCard ☐ Access ☐ American Express ☐

Card number ☐☐☐☐☐☐☐☐☐☐☐☐☐☐☐☐

Signature_____   Expiry Date_____

Name _____

Address_____

_____

_____   Postcode_____

Please send your order to: Marketing Department, Pavilion Books Ltd,
26 Upper Ground, London SE1 9PD, or fax for quick dispatch to:
Marketing Department, 0171-620 0042.